To Risk
It All

ALSO BY ADMIRAL JAMES STAVRIDIS, USN (RET.)

Sailing True North

Sea Power

The Accidental Admiral

Partnership for the Americas

Destroyer Captain

COAUTHORED BY ADMIRAL JAMES STAVRIDIS, USN (RET.)

2034: A Novel of the Next War

Command at Sea

The Leader's Bookshelf

Watch Officer's Guide

Division Officer's Guide

To Risk It All

Nine Conflicts and the Crucible of Decision

Admiral James Stavridis,
USN (Ret.)

Penguin Press *New York* 2022

PENGUIN PRESS
An imprint of Penguin Random House LLC
penguinrandomhouse.com

Photo credits
p. xxviii Engraving by Henry Bryan Hall and Sons via Naval History and Heritage Command
p. 28 Engraving by G. R. Hall, after a painting by Alonzo Chappel. Published by Johnson,
Fry & Company, New York, 1858. Naval History and Heritage Command Photograph
p. 62 Portrait by Noah Kendall Saunders via Naval History and Heritage Command
p. 94 Naval History and Heritage Command
p. 122 Official US Navy Photograph, National Archives,
via Naval History and Heritage Command
p. 148 Maurice Constant, National Archives, via Naval History and Heritage Command
p. 186 Naval History and Heritage Command
p. 216 Photo by Petty Officer 2nd Class Jonathan Nelson, US Navy
p. 242 Photo by Mass Communication Specialist Seaman Alexander Williams, US Navy

Library of Congress Cataloging-in-Publication Data
Names: Stavridis, James, author.
Title: To risk it all : nine conflicts and the crucible of decision /
Admiral James Stavridis, USN (Ret.)
Other titles: Nine conflicts and the crucible of decision
Description: New York : Penguin Press, 2022. | Includes bibliographical
references and index.
Identifiers: LCCN 2021030958 (print) | LCCN 2021030959 (ebook) |
ISBN 9780593297742 (hardcover) | ISBN 9780593297759 (ebook)
Subjects: LCSH: United States—History, Naval | United States.
Navy—History. | United States. Navy—Biography. | Leadership.
Classification: LCC E182 .S794 2022 (print) | LCC E182 (ebook) |
DDC 359.0092/273—dc23
LC record available at https://lccn.loc.gov/2021030958
LC ebook record available at https://lccn.loc.gov/2021030959]

Printed in the United States of America
1st Printing

Set in Berling LT Std
Designed by Cassandra Garruzzo Mueller

To all who decide to serve the nation
And to the love of my life, Laura,
who thankfully took a risk on me

The essence of ultimate decision remains impenetrable to the observer—often, indeed, to the decider himself. . . . There will always be the dark and tangled stretches in the decision-making process—mysterious even to those who may be most intimately involved.

JOHN F. KENNEDY[1]

CONTENTS

INTRODUCTION

In 2021, after decades of searching, undersea explorers finally found the wreck of USS *Johnston* (DD-557), one of the most famous destroyers in US naval history.[1] It sank in very deep water off the Philippine Islands, after the chaotic and heroic Battle off Samar on October 25, 1944. The warship lay at the bottom of the sea undisturbed for over seventy-five years in more than twenty thousand feet of water, making it the deepest shipwreck ever located and successfully surveyed. When it sank, it was under the command of Commander Ernest Evans, who would become the first Native American to be awarded a Medal of Honor. Ernest Evans was half Cherokee and a quarter Creek. As famed historian Rear Admiral Samuel Eliot Morison said in his iconic study of US naval operations in the Second World War, "In no engagement of its entire history has the United States Navy shown more gallantry, guts, and gumption than in those two morning hours between 0730 and 0930 off

Samar." Under the determined command of Ernest Evans, his destroyer led a seemingly suicidal charge against vastly superior Japanese warships to try to protect lightly armored carriers during the crucial moments of the Battle of Leyte Gulf. Of his crew of 329, Evans and 183 others perished in the battle or in the waters afterward.

I studied the battle many years ago as a young midshipman at Annapolis and have continued to read the many books and articles about Commander Evans and his gallant destroyer over the years.[2] Born in 1908, Evans graduated from the Naval Academy in 1931 and commanded a destroyer for the first time early in the war: USS *Alden*. After successful Pacific combat operations in *Alden*, he was selected as the commissioning commander of the new *Fletcher*-class destroyer *Johnston* in 1943, and he subsequently deployed again to the Pacific at the height of the war.

In the fall of 1944, *Johnston* was part of a small flotilla of seven destroyers (including also USS *Hoel* and USS *Samuel B. Roberts*, which were likewise sunk in combat) assigned to protect light escort aircraft carriers at Leyte Gulf under the overall command of Admiral Bull Halsey. Due to Halsey's impetuous decision to move the bulk of his Third Fleet north to chase what he thought was the main Japanese force, the small ships were all that remained between the carriers and a heavy Japanese surface force. General

Douglas MacArthur's ability to retake the Philippines and fulfill his storied pledge to return hung in the balance.

Facing twenty-three vastly larger Japanese battleships and heavy cruisers, the seven small destroyers charged to protect the flattops. The action is universally known as "the last stand of the tin can sailors," a "tin can" being an affectionate Navy nickname for a destroyer. Despite being totally outgunned, Evans made the hardest of decisions in combat: to risk it all in accomplishing his mission. He laid a smoke screen and charged at flank speed directly at the Japanese to make a torpedo attack, telling his crew over the ship's announcing system that the odds were stacked against them, but they would attack anyway to protect the rest of the force. For two hours, the tiny destroyer engaged in a series of gun battles with the much larger Japanese warships. Evans was badly wounded by Japanese shellfire, but his small ship continued the fight relentlessly. The heavy guns of the Japanese fleet— including the largest super battleship in their fleet, *Yamato*— eventually sank *Johnston* alongside several other destroyers.

The decision Evans made in the furious moments of combat off Samar—to charge a vastly stronger enemy— continues to be studied and revered in today's Navy. Even the Japanese fleet rendered honors as the small ships sank before them, and treated the survivors they recovered with respect as they were taken prisoner. And because of the heroic actions of *Johnston* and the other destroyers, the carriers were able to escape. The Japanese admiral believed the destroyers would not have charged without heavier American forces in the vicinity and withdrew in confusion. MacArthur was able to successfully land his amphibious force and free the Philippines as he had promised.

It was the pivotal moment in the most consequential battle at sea of the Second World War. The US success rested on many factors, of course, but the decision Evans made to charge the enemy, a split-second choice when the battle surged around him, was at the heart of the US victory—although it cost him his life and his ship. As I contemplated that battle again and again in the course of a long Navy career—and think about it today—I ask myself two questions.

The first is simply, What was going through Evans's mind as he gave the order to charge the Japanese fleet? Was he caught up in the bloodlust of the moment, or was he cool and serene as he maneuvered the ship and launched a spread of torpedoes? Did he think about his childhood or his family? Or was it all drowned out by the booming of the Japanese guns and the hissing rush of the water down the sides of his destroyer as it gained speed? Did he think he could get in, launch torpedoes, and somehow escape the heavy guns ahead of him? Or was it clear that his was indeed a "last stand," and he made his hard choice and shut his mind to any chance of escape?

The second question is harder to answer: Would I have had the guts to make that hardest of choices? I've seen my share of combat operations, but never anything remotely like the bleak set of options Ernest Evans had before him on that fall day in the humid waters of Leyte Gulf. When I reflect back across the long years I spent at sea in command of warships, the days of the Cold War come back into focus in this regard. In those days, we faced a vast Soviet fleet that had powerful capabilities that could challenge the US in the long cruises where we faced each other in the Mediterranean Sea, the North Atlantic (the novel *The Bedford Incident* comes to mind), the Western Pacific around the Korean Peninsula, and the Caribbean off the coast of Cuba. It was *The Hunt for Red October* often, as our aircraft and destroyers worked together to track and often "hold down" Soviet nuclear submarines.

We did that at general quarters, with all hands at their battle stations, and we knew a miscalculation could lead not only to deadly events in our immediate sea space but enormous consequences for the world. For those Cold War years, we stood the watch forward deployed, hoping a war wouldn't explode in front of us. In terms of risk, we knew the enemy had deadly capabilities in long-range cruise missiles, land-based attack aircraft, and submarines armed with nuclear torpedoes. We tried to keep a mindset of calm professionalism, knowing that we couldn't afford the luxury of reacting in anger or frustration as we tracked a relentless enemy on the long night watches. The Falklands War showed us what a war at sea would look like, and the sight of multiple British warships sunk by land-based Argentine aircraft and conversely the sinking of Argentine cruiser *Belgrano* by a British nuclear submarine were indelible images. How to balance exhaustion, risk, and geopolitical impact was the coin of the realm in deep-ocean Cold War days.

In the latter half of my career, the Navy increasingly focused on operations in the littoral waters of the Arabian Gulf, the South China Sea, and the eastern Mediterranean. From those relatively shallow and constricted waters, we sank Iranian warships after their attempts to mine the Strait of Hormuz, conducted the massive strikes of Desert Storm against Iraq, and—after 9/11—found ourselves battling terrorists "from the sea." I remember sailing through the Strait of Hormuz in the mid-1980s, watching Iranian missile sites flash their targeting radars and illuminate us with fire-control sensors. The temptation was always to strike first, but the rules of engagement dominated the decision-making process—while not required to wait for an actual missile launch to attack an enemy, the onus was on us to wait for appropriate provocation. The decision-making was excruciating, and again, the mindset had to be one part steady on the trigger, and the other part ready to lunge for the firing key. How do you balance those things?

For me, it was something I learned from the senior captains I worked for—*forcing time to slow down*. The best military decision-makers have an ability to swiftly synthesize sensor data from radars, sonars, and communication nets; mentally check it against intelligence received from the vast US surveillance system; correlate the threat; discern the intentions of the enemy; and act decisively either in suppressing fire or releasing batteries. You do that by being reasonably rested; clearing your mind of all the excess white noise (including your personal thoughts); breathing deeply and steadily; lowering your voice, never raising it; and constantly moving your field of view across the sensors and the members of the firing team arrayed in front of you. Decision-making is hard to begin with at sea—it's vastly harder if you become emotionally cluttered. Over the years, I became better at deciding things under extreme stress, and spent more time learning about other sailors who had excelled in such settings, like Medal of Honor recipient Commander Ernest Evans. All of that led me to this book.

Broadly speaking, I've always been fascinated by the idea of how we make the decisions that shape our lives. If you stop and think about it, of course, we are literally deciding things almost every minute. They can range, as the saying goes, from the sublime to the ridiculous. In a sense, we are the sum of the decisions we make, both tactically and strategically. Most of the choices are largely unconscious reactions to whatever life has thrown before us that day. But occasionally, there are really *big* decisions in front of us—whom we choose to marry, whether to take one job over another, which university to attend, when to change careers. Those big, strategic decisions are generally made with plenty of time to gather information, ponder the impact of the decision personally, solicit advice from family and mentors, test the choices logically—all the standard techniques that are part of the way we choose the most important things in our lives.

But there are times when we must decide really important things *now*, often before all the facts are at our fingertips, acting on a combination of sketchy information, historical analogy, and imperfect measurements of risk versus reward. A sudden and time-sensitive opportunity to take a chance on a new job that offers less security but more potential reward, an investment prospect to sell or purchase a particular stock or bond in a highly volatile market, a relationship resolution of the most intensely personal type when an ultimatum is delivered, or a wrenching medical choice in the small hours of the morning standing over a relative's hospital bed—all require fast decisions. The hardest are those that must be made quickly in moments of stress and crisis. That certainly happens at sea routinely, often in combat, and even in peacetime under highly stressful but noncombat conditions. Examining *that* process—truly hard choices made in the crucible of high stress—is the aim of this book.

US naval history is full of those hard choices as the story of Commander Ernest Evans illustrates. From Captain John Paul Jones at sea in the days before the American Revolution to Admiral Bull Halsey deep in the Western Pacific in the Second World War to Captain Brett Crozier of USS *Theodore Roosevelt* off the coast of Guam leading a ship infested with coronavirus in 2020, in today's Navy, we ask our naval leaders to grapple with unimaginably difficult decisions, often in the crucible of battle. Some of those decisions affect not only the lone sailors standing watch on a warship but the entire ethos of the US Navy. Over time, some of these hard choices have made significant ripples in how the Navy views itself and have impacted the most fundamental standards that underpin the entire service. There is much to learn from such choices.

This book draws on my own experiences in facing hard choices. For example, twenty years ago, a sudden surprise attack on the United States by Al Qaeda changed everything in the Pentagon, where I was assigned as a newly selected one-star rear admiral. The US Department of Defense had to reinvent itself from a lumbering, Cold War–oriented behemoth to a nimble counterterrorism war-fighting organization. It was a period of wrenching change. Narrowly missing being killed myself by the plane that hit the Pentagon, I was suddenly thrust into a newly created role as the head of the Navy's "start-up," a combat and innovation cell, code-named "Deep Blue." As a very junior member of what the British Royal Navy would call "the admiralty," I helped shepherd the efforts to change the Navy in real time, even as we launched immediate combat operations. I faced similarly difficult choices throughout my thirty-seven-year career, including as head of all military forces in Latin America and later as Supreme Allied Commander of NATO. All of that informs the book.

Most readers of this book will never have the honor, privilege, or challenge of serving as naval officers. But the sea can serve as a laboratory that can inform critical decision-making ashore. By studying the naval hard choices in this book, readers can study and learn the general rules of the road in terms of decision-making in stressful situations.

Of note, these decisions demonstrate that organizations are always shaped by important choices. How has the ethos of the US Navy changed over time, what has been the impact of these hard choices on the broader service, and what can decision-makers in *any* endeavor learn from these experiences about how to handle the hard choices life presents us? It is important to understand how decision-makers process information, weigh alternatives, connect "ends, ways, and means," and make their choices. How does the "furious pressure of combat" cause decision-makers to function differently than they do in more measured times, and what can we all learn from these stories about how we make choices in our own lives? Indeed, the Navy is in many ways a reflection of the country. In addition to what we might learn about the Navy and its evolution from these nine decisions, how have such choices reflected the nation's sense of accountability, risk, and honor more broadly?

Another important element of all this is understanding specifically what tools help those making decisions—and what tools often fail decision-makers. I have been struck again and again by the way faulty decision-making often flows from misreading or misunderstanding history. More important than immediately grasping for a past analog to a given situation is simply to begin by understanding the problem—is there a crisis? Or rather are we facing a long-term, slowly evolving pattern of failure or challenge? Being clear-eyed in evaluating where you start is key. Closely associated with this, of course, is understanding assumptions. When I worked for Secretary of Defense Donald Rumsfeld as his senior military assistant, I would often watch him grind a briefer into dust by questioning the difference between facts—what we unquestionably know—and the mere assumptions of the case. Hence the title of his memoir of that turbulent time, *Known and Unknown*. So often, what are deemed to be facts at the beginning of any high-speed decision process can, and often do, reveal themselves to be only assumptions as the plan evolves—often to our dismay. By the way, the best of those briefers—whom we finally found after a lot of candidates failed—was a burly Army colonel named Mark Milley. He was promoted general soon after and fought very successfully under my command in Afghanistan. He was someone who could make time slow down, both in a briefing room with a very aggressive secretary of defense and in the dusty valleys of Afghanistan. As I write these words, four-star general Mark Milley is the chairman of the Joint Chiefs of Staff.

Another aspect of making these life-or-death choices is how you then take action. The execution of the decision is crucial, and it will happen in real time in stressful circumstances, of course. General George S. Patton said a less than perfect plan, violently executed, will often succeed, while General Dwight Eisenhower observed that no plan survives contact with the enemy. In my experience, both were right, and finding the balance in avoiding allowing the "desire for perfect to become the enemy of good enough" is fundamental to the art of decision-making. Associated with this, of course, is measuring the *outcome* of a given choice— monitoring and metrics—which is vital. What matters and what does not must be clearly understood, and good decision-makers must avoid the seductive appeal and ultimate failure of false metrics.

Advocating and communicating the decision is often as important as generating it—understanding what just happened, developing the plan, and applying the resources smoothly and appropriately are all crucial. Part of this is knowing how a decision-maker ultimately declares success. Learning how to telegraph success, using optimism as a force multiplier in decision-making, and knowing when to "find the exit" are all key themes that echo through these choices.

Not all decisions are successful, of course. Recognizing when failure is inevitable is likewise a part of decision-making. As we say in North Florida where I am from, "sometimes you gotta know the difference between quitting and getting beat," meaning there are times when the smart decision is to fold your cards and walk—or even run—in the other direction. Another way to think about this is simply that all decisions have consequences, and almost always the hardest of choices involve the highest of risks, but also potentially the most deeply satisfying outcomes. Perspective and balance are crucial in evaluating the choices we make—and in getting the hardest decisions to come out right. That is equally true on the deck of a warship heading into combat as it is in the boardroom of a corporation or the operating room of a hospital.

To Risk It All is a historical meditation on the nature of decision-making under stress, an examination of the evolution of the US Navy over the course of its 250-year voyage, and a resource for any reader who must make hard decisions in his or her work and life. It is also a chance for you to come to know nine extraordinary sailors, each of whom was placed in the crucible of decision.

Why nine choices in the book, you may ask? While there's no definitive answer to that question, I did have an image in mind, consistent with the theme that decision-making can be hard and painful: in the nautical world of the seventeenth and eighteenth centuries, and indeed into the nineteenth, the corporal punishment administered at sea—when someone made a bad decision, so to speak—was flogging. And flogging was done with "the cat" or the cat-o'-nine-tails. Each of nine long lashes also had knots tied into its length and occasionally something hard and unyielding (bone or metal) attached at the end, to make the experience as painful as possible. A typical punishment might be a dozen strokes, as much more than that did sometimes permanent damage to a man's back. This punishment was given for offenses ranging from striking an officer to extreme drunkenness. Very occasionally, longer bouts of flogging were administered, perhaps for mutiny or sodomy, and the outcomes were always very painful and sometimes fatal. So, as I thought about a number of cases to include, the idea of the cat was in the back of my mind—with its nine fateful tails. Hopefully, your decisions will be well made and there will not be a painful outcome—but at times there will be. Accepting that decisions have real consequences is, at the end, the essence of decision itself.

These nine sailors made the hard decisions that shaped their own lives and careers, resulted in a wide range of operational outcomes, and shifted the way our Navy looks at itself. They also provide a vivid tapestry of skills and instincts that comprise the essence of decision-making. All of us will face hard choices in the voyage of our lives—some in important and public ways, others in the quiet hours around the kitchen table. Business, finance, medicine, education, public policy, and a thousand other fields of endeavor all require the ability to decide quickly and well. I hope and believe that by spending some time with these nine sailors, your ability to make the hard choices in the crucible of life—whatever the circumstances—will improve.

Let's get underway.

CHAPTER ONE

The Power of "No"

———•———

Captain John Paul Jones, Continental Navy

Commander of Continental Navy Ship
Bonhomme Richard

THE BATTLE OF FLAMBOROUGH HEAD

SEPTEMBER 23, 1779

Give me a fast ship, for I intend to go in harm's way.

ATTRIBUTED TO JOHN PAUL JONES

When I walked into the United States Naval Academy on a hot summer's day in the early 1970s, the first thing that happened to me was that I got a quick and brutal haircut. It was not only a sudden induction into military life but a way for the Navy to emphasize that my own power to decide anything, including the length of my hair, was emphatically terminated. Alongside twelve hundred classmates from every state in the Union and a smattering of foreign countries, we were then lined up in a very rough formation, broken into small groups—squads of about a dozen—and marched around the Academy grounds. The highlight of those first hours was an introduction to Captain John Paul Jones, or, more accurately, to his crypt in the heart of the massive Naval Academy Chapel—the de facto high church of the US Navy.

When it came our turn to enter the chapel and see the

crypt, my squad was ordered to maintain complete "silence about the decks" and remove our "covers" (little blue-striped sailor hats, or "Dixie cups" as they were called with extreme derision by the upper-class midshipmen who were shepherding us around). We were then shuffled into the relatively small crypt, at the center of which repose the earthly remains of John Paul Jones. At that time, I had little knowledge of Jones beyond a schoolboy's appreciation for his immortal words "I have not yet begun to fight," supposedly uttered at the climax of a bloody Revolutionary War sea battle conducted off the eastern coast of the United Kingdom. Later I would discover that the saying—memorized along with other bon mots from Jones by generations of midshipmen—was almost certainly apocryphal. But at that moment, in the crypt, I was at least happy to be out of the humid summer haze of Annapolis and in some air conditioning.

We were arrayed in a loose circle around the crypt at "parade rest," and one of the senior midshipmen read a lengthy passage on Jones and his contributions to the Navy and the nation. It was full of heroic pronouncements about overcoming fearful odds in battle again and again, quotes about the qualities and characteristics of a naval officer, and lots of commentary concerning command at sea. At the time, I found it quite inspiring, and later that evening pulled out the small booklet we were given upon arrival, *Reef Points*, and began to memorize some of Jones's sayings and exploits. This scene has played out many thousands of times as young midshipmen arrive at the Academy and begin their voyages in the Navy and Marine Corps, and ultimately set their course to go to sea and join the fleet. It is not an exaggeration to say that John Paul Jones is in many ways "the father of the American Navy." I learned of him on the first day of my naval life, and he was a part of my own life at sea, both in peace and at war, for almost forty years.

As I matured and learned more about this complicated, difficult sailor and sea captain, my initial admiration for his legend diminished somewhat. I began to understand the dark side of John Paul Jones—the immense vanity, deep insecurity, sexual profligacy, and enormous ambition that drove this gardener's son who seemed cursed with an inferiority complex. He had a vicious temper that would flare often at sea, and his men at times suffered as a result. Jones was no Vice Admiral Horatio Nelson nor a Fleet Admiral Chester Nimitz, the beau ideals of naval leadership.[1] He lacked their ability to inspire subordinates and build a band of brothers who could fight together and win decisively. Jones ended his days a broken man, nearly destitute, living a hardscrabble existence in Paris and dying at the age of forty-five a largely unmourned and forgotten figure.

But at the heart of this compact, handsome man was an indomitable fighting spirit. He was a superb mariner who knew the sea well and could bring to bear his knowledge of ship-handling in the complex age of sail, his gunnery and boarding tactics, and his keen sense of when an opponent might be faltering. His personal courage was remarkable and frequently deployed in combat. Jones was a classic sea warrior willing to lead from the front—whether in close boarding fights, personally aiming a cannon, or subduing a mutinous subordinate. Despite his small size (he was about my height, a not-so-towering five foot six), he had the kind of courage that made him seem larger than life in a fight.

Ashore, however, he was typically quiet, a bit subdued, and strove to appear very much the gentleman. Abigail Adams, in a brilliant turn of phrase, once said, "He is small of stature. . . . I should sooner think of wrapping him up in cotton wool and putting him into my pocket, than sending him to contend with cannon ball[s]."[2] Indeed, his love life was quite fulsome and a source of satisfaction to Jones, although the tumultuous course of his life ultimately precluded a marriage. He indulged in one torrid affair after another but told companions again and again that he was not one to settle down with a single woman—despite his occasional propensity to pour his heart out in poorly written love poetry.[3] With a handsome head of dark hair, sharply etched cheekbones, and an athletic mien, Jones never lacked for female companionship.

Born in southwest Scotland on July 6, 1747, he grew up on a large estate called Arbigland as the son of the head gardener, John Paul Sr.; Jones was named John Paul Jr. after his father, and added the "Jones" only later in life. I visited the estate when I was Supreme Allied Commander of NATO and noticed that it affords sweeping views of the sea, which must have inspired Jones early. He set sail as a young teen, in an era when life at sea was truly like "being in a jail, with the chance of being drowned," in the memorable words of Samuel Johnson. As was customary, he began as an apprentice— essentially a midshipman—to learn the ropes, quite literally, in sailing ships. The early part of his seagoing days was spent in a series of merchant and slave ships, and he sailed the North Atlantic passages frequently.

He became a sea captain for the first time unexpectedly in 1768 when the brig in which he was sailing as a mate, the *John*, lost both the captain and the first mate. John Paul was able to get the ship safely back into port, and the Scottish owners rewarded him with his first command. His propensity for harsh discipline was then unfettered as he ascended to become a ship's captain, which in the eighteenth century was an office imbued with immense power. This led in 1770 to a highly publicized flogging and the eventual death of one of his crew members (who had strong influence in Scotland via family connections), for which John Paul was arrested and investigated. While released on bail, he was able to gather enough evidence to exonerate himself, but the incident had a lasting negative effect both on his reputation in Scotland and upon his own prickly sense of self-worth. It also led him to depart Scotland and strike out more broadly in the world. This strategy seems to have worked, as John Paul was given another command soon thereafter, this time of a London-based West Indiaman called the *Betsy*. John Paul again had to put down a rebellious crew member, killing him in a "disagreement" over wages. He now left England under a cloud as well, coming to Virginia and settling near Fredericksburg. Here he adopted the surname Jones to distance himself from the unsavory stories that followed on from his brushes with the law.[4]

So it was John Paul *Jones* who volunteered his services to the Continental Navy in 1775, around the time the fledgling Navy and Marine Corps were founded. His first ship was a twenty-four-gun frigate, *Alfred*, to which he was posted as the first lieutenant toward the end of that year. Of note, he had the honor of raising the so-called Grand Union Flag at the mast of the ship—perhaps the first time a US flag was flown in a warship.[5] While his time in *Alfred* was relatively short, he was quickly able to gain command of a sloop of war, the *Providence*, in 1776. While in his first warship command role, he undertook essentially logistic duties, ferrying supplies from Continental bases to depots closer to troops in the field, and moving soldiers to and from assembly points. Yet he was still able to capture more than a dozen prizes and continue to build his reputation in the small naval force. He returned to *Alfred* as the captain in the fall of that year, but a dispute with the Continental Navy's leadership resulted in his being given a smaller and less prestigious command, the sloop *Ranger*, in 1777.

Ranger ultimately provided a significant boost to Jones's career in the American Navy. It also led to his improbable and lasting friendship with Benjamin Franklin when the two worked together in France following the Treaty of Alliance between the United States and France in 1778, where Franklin was one of the US commissioners to that nation. It is hard to summon a mental picture of these two mismatched friends strolling through eighteenth-century Paris, but they remained warmly supportive of each other throughout their lives. Franklin was even instrumental in arranging for the *Ranger* to become the first US warship to receive a formal salute from France. Jones departed that nation in spring of 1778 to conduct a campaign of maritime guerrilla warfare (which the English regarded as simple piracy) on the British towns and shipping along the coast of the Irish Sea.

While he constantly complained about the low quality of his officers and crew, he was ultimately able to bind them into a somewhat effective if undisciplined raiding force. They conducted a series of operations along the English coast, mostly directed against an increasingly terrified civilian population. The British press of this time depicted Jones repeatedly as a privateer, and on several occasions his crew did in fact avail themselves of booty and liquor ashore. The apex of *Ranger's* war cruise was a single-ship engagement with a roughly equally armed British man-of-war, HMS *Drake*. On April 24, 1778, the two ships fought, and Jones was the victor, a milestone for the nascent US Navy. The victory was later tarnished by a dispute between Jones and his first mate (the reoccurring pattern of failing to control his subordinates) that had to be adjudicated by John Adams, then also a US commissioner in France. Nonetheless, the fight stands as one of the earliest victories at sea by a US warship, and was particularly important given that it was a win over the vaunted Royal Navy.[6]

By 1779, Jones was given command of a larger, albeit slow and occasionally unseaworthy, vessel, the forty-two-gun United States Ship *Bonhomme Richard*. She was a reconfigured merchant ship given to the Americans by the French. A sluggish sea-keeper but heavily armed, the ship would eventually make the fighting reputation that followed Jones for the remainder of his seagoing life. With the help of Ben Franklin who provided cash and contacts, Jones broke his flag aboard the ship as a commodore in command of a small squadron of mismatched ships led by an eclectic mix of captains: tiny twelve-gun USS *Vengeance*, thirty-six-gun USS *Alliance* (commanded by an eccentric and spectacularly unreliable French captain, Pierre Landais), and thirty-two-gun USS *Pallas*. He also had two privateers in company, with French crews. The British were aware of the squadron's existence and general plan (having watched Jones during his adventures in *Ranger*) and sent a small group of warships to intercept him and protect coastal convoys in the area. As was the usual case for Jones, he had extreme difficulty controlling his subordinates, particularly Captain Landais in the ironically named *Alliance*. Jones decided to sail farther north into the North Sea, then down the eastern coast of Britain, searching for prizes and generally harassing the British.

By September 23, 1779, the small squadron was off the coast of Flamborough Head near East Yorkshire, where Jones herded his vessels together in the early-morning hours. Here he encountered a British Baltic convoy of around four ships with rich merchant cargoes of iron and timber headed to various southern English ports. Unfortunately for Jones, there were also two British warships in the vicinity. The larger and more capable warship was the forty-four-gun HMS *Serapis*, and she was escorted by the smaller twenty-two-gun *Countess of Scarborough*, essentially a contracted combatant (not a Royal Navy vessel, but still quite capable). Together, they had the mission of protecting the convoy from predators like the Americans and French. By 4:00 p.m., the two British ships had managed to maneuver themselves into a blocking position to protect the merchant ships. HMS *Serapis* was commanded by Captain Richard Pearson.

By 6:00 p.m., Jones had conceived his battle plan and had *Bonhomme Richard* and *Alliance* in a loose formation headed toward the British. At this point, Captain Landais began to deviate from Jones's plan, using the better sailing qualities of his newer and faster frigate to split the two British ships. This left *Bonhomme Richard* and the other smaller American ships to fight the larger and more dangerous *Serapis*, while *Alliance* was matched against the much smaller *Countess of Scarborough*. After an initial query from the British to the Americans, the two sides traded broadsides beginning around 7:15 p.m.

As the battle unfolded over the next several hours, it became clear that despite having more total gunnery capability among his four principal ships, Jones was handicapped by several factors. First was the intransigence of the French captain Landais, who simply ignored Jones's orders throughout much of the engagement. Second, his forces never effectively operated as a single cohesive unit, lacking as they did a unified plan of engagement, which Jones—ever the individualist—failed to provide. And third, the crews of both *Serapis* and the *Countess of Scarborough* were much more professional and better trained for the kind of confused night combat that ensued.

As a result, the first round of the battle—especially the evolving one-on-one combat between *Bonhomme Richard* and *Serapis*—went largely to the British. Jones realized he was outgunned and decided to try to ram, grapple, and board his opponent. The British were able to pour several rounds of cannon fire into Jones's ship, using the better maneuverability of *Serapis,* including raking *Bonhomme Richard* around 7:30 p.m. The devastation to the old merchant ship was enormous—scores of both Marines and sailors were killed, much of the ship's main battery of cannon were destroyed, and the American ship was holed below the waterline in several places.

The British captain closed in for the kill at roughly 8:00 p.m.—but Jones was able to take advantage of the wind dying and stalling *Serapis,* leaving her "in irons" momentarily.

This was the moment when John Paul Jones rammed his opponent and attempted to board and carry her away. Unfortunately, his boarding plan initially failed as the two ships drifted apart. His next maneuver, at roughly 8:30 p.m., was to take advantage of being to windward of *Serapis* to deliver his own raking broadside. This had little overall effect on the fight due to the damage already sustained by his sinking ship, where the crews to man the main guns were mostly hors de combat. At this point, the deck of *Bonhomme Richard* looked like a scene from Dante's *Inferno*—a mass of mangled bodies, bloody and exploded cannon, and burnt sails and masts. By 9:00 p.m., Jones had only his small quarterdeck guns left in action.

Serapis was not in greatly better condition but was still far more functional in terms of sailing and firing its big guns than Jones's ship. On the other side of the maritime battlefield, Jones's smaller companion, *Pallas*, was gamely attacking *Countess of Scarborough*, but Jones could not find the errant *Alliance* within the night horizon and cursed Landais's intransigence. Suddenly, at roughly 9:15 p.m., both *Bonhomme Richard* and *Serapis* were raked with grapeshot. Landais had chosen to reappear and fire indiscriminately into the hot mess of the two conjoined warships. After delivering two brutal volleys, killing both British and Americans on their respective ships, he disengaged and again slipped into the dark night. By this point, it was increasingly clear that *Bonhomme Richard* was probably going to sink. Jones himself was utterly exhausted, and his men seemed to lose heart, with several of them calling out for quarter from the British ship.

This was the point in the battle where virtually any other captain would have "struck his colors," or hauled down his flag and surrendered. This was considered an honorable and sensible thing to do under such circumstances, and on Jones's battered warship, his crew clearly wanted him to do so. Understandably enough considering the general confusion of the smoking firefight, the precise timing of exchanges about surrender remain unclear. But most sources agree that around 10:00 p.m., some of Jones's surviving officers— including possibly his Marine lieutenant—shouted a verbal surrender to the British ship. Jones exploded with fury, throwing a pistol at one of his officers who was headed to the mainmast to take down the colors.[7] The British captain, having heard the shouts for quarter, inquired if Jones intended to surrender. At this moment, Jones's reply became the most memorable line of his life. It has come down to us, unreliably, as "I have not yet begun to fight." We cannot be certain of the exact construction of his rebuttal, but it was certainly a strongly worded negative—more likely it was something such as, "I will make YOU strike first." It seems probable there might have been a few expletives included, for the battle fever was running high in Jones. Another version that has come down from a contemporary was, "I may sink, but I'll be damned if I strike."[8] Regardless of the exact wording, the intent was clear, and the battle continued.

Let's step into the mind of Commodore John Paul Jones at this pivotal moment. He did not leave a detailed version of his inner thoughts, but having commanded ships in combat situations I would guess that two parallel emotions were swirling through his head. First, and most obviously, there was the high fever and emotion of the fight. Jones had spent much of his early years building a reputation as a competent seaman and fighting captain. He would have been genuinely angry at the prospect of all of it collapsing, especially at the hands of the aristocratic British Royal Navy. His choice essentially became "you may kill me, but you cannot diminish me or my place in the world." Anger drove that part of his calculus, a reminder that in the direst of situations, our emotions can provide a powerful spur to action. But my suspicion is that another part of Jones's mind was at play in the decision calculus, and it was here that he was processing the odds before him and calculated that his men needed to see their captain fight in bitter and uncompromising actions. That combination of emotion and calculation—and the need to find the balance—is a pattern we will see again and again.

Jones continued the fight, his temper high, shouting at his crew over the thunder of the big guns and the relentless crackle of musket fire directed from the upper platforms of what remained of the masts. The unhelpful *Alliance* continued to dip in and out of the battle, returning around 10:15 p.m. to unload another ill-aimed broadside that further damaged both of the combatants. Events were dire on the clearly sinking *Bonhomme Richard*, but in all the confusion, luckily for Jones, Captain Pearson of *Serapis* could not understand the extent of the wounds to the old merchantman.

Casualties on both ships were approaching 50 percent killed and wounded (an extraordinarily bloody total in the age of sail). Not realizing the extent of the damage to his principal opponent and cognizant of the presence of the essentially unharmed *Alliance*, the British captain capitulated. Pearson chose to strike his colors around 10:30 p.m. Despite further confusion and some lingering casualties, this effectively ended the most iconic sea battle of the Revolutionary War. The merchant convoy that Pearson sought to protect made its way out of the area of the battle and continued on to safety, perhaps another factor in Pearson's decision to strike his colors. Reflecting the severe physical beating she had taken in the battle, *Bonhomme Richard* sank the next morning despite the Americans' best efforts to keep her afloat. Jones departed with Pearson's ceremonial sword and a handful of prize ships, setting sail to the Netherlands in them. Jones had made the right choice, found the balance between roaring anger and cold calculation, and won an improbable and memorable fight at sea.

The victory over *Serapis* was the highlight of Jones's naval career, and certainly of his service in the Continental Navy. He was feted on both sides of the Atlantic and named a chevalier (knight) of France by Louis XVI. He remained nominally in the nascent American Navy for the next several years and was appointed to command the seventy-four-gun USS *America* in 1782. Unfortunately for Jones, this vessel was handed over to the French as reparations for debts incurred in the war, and by 1783 he was back in Paris trying to collect outstanding prize money for his crew. Eventually his string of naval service ran out with the United States, and he entered the service of Empress Catherine II of Russia, making him a trivia quiz answer as the only individual who served as an American commodore and a Russian admiral in the history of the two countries. To his credit, he did retain his American citizenship, probably as a hedge if things went less than well—which, of course, they did.

In the Russian Navy, he commanded a twenty-four-gun ship, the *Vladimir*, and fought in several campaigns against the Turks with little fanfare or real success. In addition to resentments from other international sea captains in

Catherine's employ (notably the British, who regarded him as little more than a pirate), there was a sex scandal that he was caught up in—he was accused of raping a twelve-year-old girl. The charges appear to have been trumped up, and he eventually overcame the possibility of a legal conviction, but any hope of further advancement in the Russian Navy was over. By the summer of 1789, he left for a brief hiatus in Poland before landing in Paris in 1790.

While still nominally a Russian rear admiral with a small pension, Jones had no further prospect of returning to Catherine's court and getting back to sea in command—although he continued to send imploring letters to the empress from Paris. He had a final diplomatic appointment to represent the United States before the court of the Dey (governor) of Algiers with the hope of winning the release of American prisoners in 1792, but he died before he could undertake this final, strange mission. Jones died at the age of forty-five on July 18, 1792, regarded at the end as a man of courage and seagoing skill, but also possessed of an overweening ego consumed by ambitions he never fulfilled. His body was buried in the St. Louis Cemetery in Paris, which itself was paved over some decades later. That, it seemed, was the end of the voyage.

But in one of the oddest postscripts in naval history, Jones was exhumed in 1905 at the urging of President

Theodore Roosevelt, who was enthralled with the legends of Jones's bravery in combat and looking for a symbol for the global Navy he wanted to create. It took six years to search down the body's location, as the cemetery's land had been put to other uses, but Jones's "luck" held in that he'd been preserved in alcohol and sealed in a lead-lined coffin.

Once exhumed, his body sailed in state on USS *Brooklyn*, with an escort of three other ships of the line, all American cruisers. As the four cruisers approached the Virginia coast, seven battleships joined the convoy to complete the homecoming. On April 24, 1906, he was interred again at the US Naval Academy at a ceremony personally presided over by President Roosevelt, his remains eventually installed in 1913 in the magnificent crypt beneath the magisterial chapel visited by Midshipman Stavridis nearly seventy years later.

No matter how history regards John Paul Jones and ultimately measures his qualities as a leader, mariner, and tactician, it is the singular decision he made off Flamborough Head to continue a seemingly lost battle for which he will be principally remembered. His ship was clearly sinking under his feet, nearly half his crew killed and wounded, his small flotilla confused and pouring in friendly fire, and his sailors so demoralized as to attempt to surrender the ship without his consent. Yet despite all of this—in an era in which there was no shame in surrendering to a more powerful foe, which

Serapis clearly represented—Jones chose to reply defiantly and fight on. Whatever the exact wording of his retort, it was a brutally hard decision to make, and has been memorialized (and memorized) by generations of naval officers. What went into the decision?

Clearly, Jones thought that tactically he could still win the battle, but there was certainly a significant psychological component to his choice. Part of why he believed he could ultimately triumph is probably attributable to his experiences in other combat actions during his life, but also to an intense internal sense of his own innate talent and indomitability. Throughout his life, he was a scrappy, undersized fighter who was unwilling to let larger and better endowed opponents defeat him. Jones suffered from a common complex that many small men have, which is that they are driven by the need to show themselves "as big as anyone." The son of a blue-collar gardener who saw himself as gentleman sea captain and maritime warrior, Jones was truly loath to lose a fight to an elegant British sea captain. Insecurity is a spur that drives many people, and the need to prove oneself is often buried deep and early. Jones's early years seem to have put a big, smoking hole in his psyche, and he spent his entire life trying to fill it—with women conquered, sea battles won, commands undertaken, floggings given, and titles bestowed. Yet that hole was never filled—it never is—and the decision to fight on in a hopeless moment was a manifestation of his psychology more than any brilliant tactical calculus. There were deep personal psychological currents pulsing through Jones, and a lethal combat scenario brought those to the fore, leading to a vivid decision—to say no to surrendering the ship.

But it is simplistic to say that the decision to refuse a logical surrender was only a foregone conclusion of his psychology. There are other aspects to the events off Flamborough Head that have echoed through the US Navy and indeed the American way of war for 250 years. Perhaps the most accurate depiction of what must have flashed through Jones's mind as he formulated his choice is what is called today an "OODA loop." Articulated by the highly regarded military strategist and retired US Air Force colonel John Boyd, OODA stands for "observe—orient—decide—act." It is an approach to decision-making under stress, originally part of training fighter pilots for dogfights. A combatant must begin by observing, and doing so quickly and cleanly, avoiding prejudices and misinformation. He or she would next orient the information, applying culture, previous experience, and analytic tools. This is the most important of the four steps of the loop, and precedes the decision moment, which is naturally followed by acting.

The key to understanding the OODA loop is that all four

of the steps are constantly in progress in any decision, but especially in the high-speed tempo of combat. For Captain Jones, his observations were very much in the moment, with his ship shot to hell, the mast falling, crewmembers moaning in agony around him, dense smoke filling the air, and errant gunshots from his "partner" *Alliance* incoming. Almost any other captain would have struck his colors at that moment, and events were trending in that direction given the missteps of Jones's own crew in attempting to strike. But Jones oriented and at that moment applied to the situation his aggressive personality, personal experience, deep emotion and ambition, and the culture of the upstart American nation. He quickly then made a seemingly unorthodox decision to continue fighting and acted upon it. In all of Colonel Boyd's writing, he emphasizes that victory in combat accrues to the decision-maker who can "get inside the decision loop" of his or her opponent. This is precisely what happened in the climactic moment of the battle—Jones, despite having the weaker hand of cards, was moving more quickly to assess the situation (observe), analyze where the combat process was moving (orient), make swift choices (decide), and execute those decisions (act). In this process, Jones anticipated the celebrated OODA loop developed by Colonel John Boyd two centuries later to categorize airborne fighter combat. In essence, Jones was "turning inside" the decision loop of his opponent, Captain Pearson. And it made all the difference, meaning he was observing/orienting/deciding/acting much more quickly.

Decisions made in combat are perhaps the hardest of hard choices for a host of obvious reasons. The life-or-death stakes, the national implications of victory or defeat, the bonds with fellow combatants, and the heightened emotions generated by a close fight simply provide a different and sharper context to any choice a decision-maker takes. In combat, most observers have a sense of time slowing down. Whenever I have been in a dangerous situation, from operations in the Arabian Gulf at sea or ashore in Afghanistan, I have consciously felt the steady ticktock of events slow and tried at such moments to rely on training and instincts, sublimating emotion. But this is precisely where the power of "no," the releasing energy of simple defiance, the primal internal scream of refusing to be defeated, no matter the odds, deeply matters. Think of Winston Churchill, that most emphatic of decision-makers, and his famous quote: "Never give in. Never give in. Never, never, never, never—in nothing, great or small, large or petty—never give in, except to convictions of honor and good sense. Never yield to force. Never yield to the apparently overwhelming might of the enemy."[9] An American could be forgiven for thinking that Sir Winston was simply channeling the complicated

American naval hero John Paul Jones. The power of "no" continues to be part of some of the hardest decisions we must make.

Jones's actions on that day formed a major part of the ethos of the fledgling US Navy, and have been part of the bedrock of the service for well over two centuries. The received wisdom of John Paul Jones is packaged into his crypt at Annapolis, the dozens of books about him, the warships that have borne both his name and his flagship's (including a formidable *Arleigh Burke*–class guided missile destroyer that sails with the fleet today, alongside a massive amphibious assault ship, *Bonhomme Richard*),* and film appearances. You can drop a plumb line from his words in *Bonhomme Richard* to the behavior of our sea captains on hundreds of warships at sea today. To understand the Navy's immensely judgmental reaction to Lieutenant Commander Lloyd Bucher's surrender of USS *Pueblo*, you must begin with the victory won by John Paul Jones. We will examine Bucher's terrible dilemma in a later chapter of this book.

Turn back for a moment to young and recently shorn Midshipman Stavridis in that nicely air-conditioned crypt in Annapolis so many years ago. I looked in awe at the beautiful

---

* Sadly, the massive USS *Bonhomme Richard* caught fire in a San Diego shipyard as she was finishing a very expensive overhaul and burned much of her superstructure in the summer of 2020. The cost of repairing her was deemed excessive, and she was decommissioned and subsequently scrapped.

black marble, and the scenes of battle ringed around it, and something of the spirit of that scrappy captain found its way into my own heart, and it resides there today. Fortunately for me, I never faced the kind of wrenching choice that John Paul Jones did on the deck of *Bonhomme Richard* in her extravagant death throes. But I believe that his obstinate determination to fight through every obstacle, no matter the cost, is still very much part of the ethos of our Navy. This is not to say we embark on suicide missions out of anger and hubris; rather that we harness the violence of the moment and couple it to calculation, finding a course to sail in even the most challenging seas. At its best, that is the "Navy way" in a fight at sea.

It certainly informed my approach at a wide variety of moments in my own career, from standing in a smoking Pentagon in the wake of the 9/11 attacks, to sailing under Iranian missiles in the Arabian Gulf as a rear admiral, to struggling with terrible combat losses in Afghanistan as Supreme Allied Commander of NATO. And it informs the fleet today, years after I have sailed on to civilian life. We will fail at times as a service, and have fallen short in one incident or another, certainly. Such is the nature of sailing in challenging seas, and that is a pretty good lesson for all of us sailing the voyages of our lives, whatever our profession. Despite all his foibles and personal missteps, John Paul Jones left us with a powerful gift: the spirit of determination that is still very much at the heart of our Navy and is part of our national spirit as well. At our best, we still have the power of "no," of saying, in the simplest terms, that we will not give up the ship—never, never, never—no matter the cost, so long as we have the means to resist.

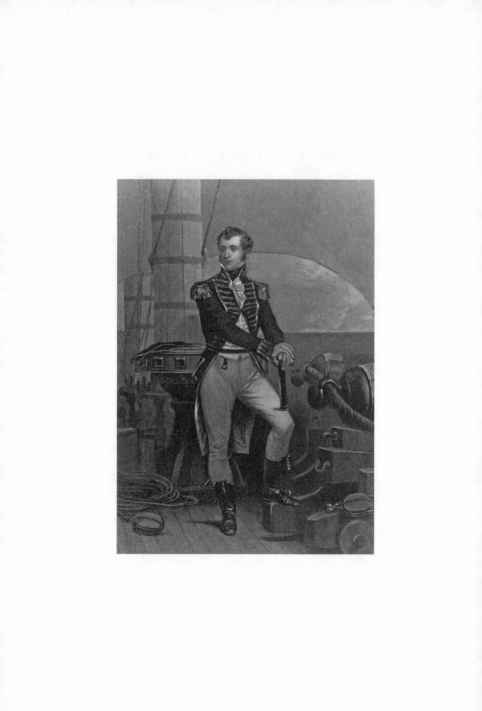

CHAPTER TWO

A Young Man's Game

———◆———

Lieutenant Stephen Decatur, United States Navy
Commander of USS Intrepid, *a Four-Gun Ketch*

CUTTING-OUT EXPEDITION IN TRIPOLI
HARBOR, BARBARY STATES,
NORTH AFRICA

FEBRUARY 16, 1804

Hesitation increases in relation to risk
in equal proportion to age.

ERNEST HEMINGWAY[1]

I came to truly know the story of Stephen Decatur late in life—well into my early forties—because I was assigned to write a speech while attached to the Joint Staff in the Pentagon. Immediately after departing command of destroyer USS *Barry* in late 1995, I had arrived for a tour in the Directorate for Strategy, Plans, and Policy in early 1996. I knew I would only be there for about two years and was determined to make the most of it in terms of spending time with my family after long deployments as a sea captain. I was buried deep in the policy branch of the organization, and trying to keep my head down, when I got a call from the executive assistant to the chairman of the Joint Chiefs in early May of 1997. The chairman at the time was a fascinating and inspirational officer, John Shalikashvili, universally known as General Shali. He was an immigrant whose family had come to the United States from Poland in 1952, and he spoke not only Polish but Russian and German as well. He had served briefly as Supreme Allied Commander at NATO before being selected chairman of the Joint Chiefs of Staff by President Bill Clinton.

I had been called to his office to receive an assignment to write a speech for him, the commencement speech of Harvey Mudd College in Southern California, to be delivered in mid-May of that year. After being ushered into the chairman's august presence by his executive officer, Captain (and later four-star admiral) Harry Ulrich, I was given a few words of guidance delivered in a soft, accented voice. The chairman wanted to speak about risk, and youth, and the energy that goes with those qualities. It shouldn't be a long speech, and ought to have an inspirational character or two in it—"Tell someone's story," Ulrich said. As I walked out with Captain Ulrich, he said, "Don't screw it up, Stavridis. I need a draft Friday morning early." It was Wednesday afternoon.

I began to think about inspirational characters and the quality of risks we are willing to take, and about being young. At the time, as someone who had just turned forty, "young" described someone who was in their early twenties, which I thought would be a good fit with the students at the school. And I thought I could get the broad-minded and cosmopolitan General Shali to use a Navy "character," so the idea of Stephen Decatur popped into my head. In those pre-Wikipedia days, I headed out to the United States Naval Institute in Annapolis for an afternoon, and also walked over to the Naval Academy Museum. At that point, all I knew about Stephen Decatur was that he had fought in the Barbary Wars in the early nineteenth century, where he had done some heroic things; had a series of Navy ships named for him (the fifth and current one is an *Arleigh Burke*–class destroyer); and had died at the relatively youthful age of forty-one (my age as I struggled with the speech) in a duel. But over the next forty-eight hours, I learned a great deal and came to admire more deeply this dashing officer who died far too young on what was then called the "field of chance."

The speech was a success, and General Shali sent me a gracious handwritten note of thanks, something I cherish today. But it was that deep dive into Stephen Decatur's utterly remarkable life and death that has stayed with me. When I think of him, I think of how often he took immense personal risk, from the cutting-out expedition of USS *Philadelphia* as a lieutenant in his very first command to his not infrequent and ultimately fatal duels. "Cutting out" is a term to describe a tactic commonly used in the early 1800s when a large ship was attacked and boarded by sailors, often at night from small boats. What alchemy of patriotism, ambition, and the strongest sense of personal honor drove him? And above all, how did he make the decision to lead a band of volunteer seamen on an incredibly risky mission to cut out the *Philadelphia*? What must have gone through his mind in those heady moments on board the hulking frigate when it became evident he couldn't get away with the ship he had just seized and would have to burn her as she swayed at her moorings in the dark North African night? For the rest of my naval career, there were times when Decatur would pop up before my eyes as I contemplated the missions I was considering for the sailors under my command, and I kept a small lithograph of him in my office. It hangs in my office today as I write these words. There was something bold and right and pure about Stephen Decatur that deeply inspired the Navy of his day, and I believe it has translated into the daring we see at times even in missions in this twenty-first century— from SEAL teams in close combat to aviators flying in storms over enemy targets and the surface Navy's boarding parties operating from the decks of our destroyers in the Arabian Gulf. We owe a debt to Decatur that is immense and real and is above all intertwined with a willingness to take risk.

Although he did not get his start in the Navy as early as David Farragut (whom I write about in chapter 3), Stephen Decatur Jr. was, if such a thing exists, a naval prodigy.

Between receiving his midshipman's commission at age nineteen and his untimely and much-mourned death at age forty-one in a duel with fellow naval officer James Barron, Decatur shone—as a well-rounded Navy officer, as a seagoing warrior, and as a living example of the fighting spirit of the growing United States Navy. Like an athlete whose career comes to define a franchise, Decatur is widely remembered and celebrated in (and beyond) today's Navy because he emerged at a time when the founding legends and standards of the service had yet to be established. He then spent two decades setting and raising the bar for his peers and all of us to follow. In a certain sense, all of us who served in today's Navy sail in the wake of Stephen Decatur. Like Babe Ruth or Bart Starr, Decatur defined the culture for all those who followed with his personality and character. But, of course, the stakes for which he played were not simply winning a ball game but risking life and limb for the nation's interest.

Three trends defined Decatur's life and times: the emergence of the United States as a player on the world stage in its own right, the birth (in earnest) of the US Navy, and the culture of honor and glory that pervaded the ranks of gentlemen in general and naval officers in particular. In recent years, the Broadway play *Hamilton* has reintroduced modern society to this culture, and there are echoes of Alexander Hamilton's ambition, honor, and ultimate doom in

Decatur's life. Honor was all, physical risk was a daily part of life, and burnishing a reputation that would outlive the moment was the ultimate objective. In this regard, there is a direct line from the ancient Greeks around the walls of Troy—endlessly striving for glory and the eternal reputation granted an Achilles or a Ulysses—to the warrior culture of Decatur's time.

Decatur was born on January 5, 1779, in the midst of the American Revolution. His parents, Stephen Sr. and Ann, lived in Philadelphia but fled the city before young Stephen's birth in the face of attacking Redcoats. They relocated to Sinepuxent, on the Eastern Shore of Maryland, where Ann gave birth to Stephen while her husband went to sea to take the fight back to the British. After the war, the Decatur family reunited in Philadelphia—a burgeoning port for the new country. Neither parent wanted the younger Stephen to follow his father to sea, but fate intervened early. At the age of eight, the boy came down with a serious case of whooping cough, for which salt air and sea breezes were thought to be a curative. Stephen Sr. brought his son along on a merchant voyage to Europe and back; upon their return, the younger Decatur was indeed cured of his cough but thoroughly infected with the love of ships and the sea.

Stephen Sr. and Ann, still hoping for their son to join the Episcopal priesthood, were not so quickly converted to

Stephen Jr.'s new dream. The young Decatur was enrolled at the prestigious Episcopal Academy in Pennsylvania, where he proved to be a distracted and none-too-diligent student. Nevertheless, he was accepted to the newly established University of Pennsylvania, where he seems to have pursued his schoolwork somewhat more rigorously—for one year. Stephen Jr. left university at age seventeen, and with his parents finally determined that if they could not keep their son from the sea, they could at least support him in his chosen career. In the first of several key interventions, Decatur's father arranged a job for him with the Philadelphia shipwrights Gurney and Smith, who were then at work building a ship that would figure in several defining episodes of Decatur's career.

The USS *United States*, then under construction in Gurney and Smith's yards, was one of the famous "six frigates" authorized by Congress in March 1794.[2] The Constitution of the United States, ratified six years previously, directed Congress to "maintain a Navy," but what exactly that should look like in practice was a matter of fierce debate in the young and indebted nation eager to spread its wings in trade while still avoiding "foreign entanglements," as George Washington counseled. Northerners, whose economy depended so heavily on maritime trade, pushed early and strongly for a permanent navy strong enough to defend a burgeoning shipping industry no longer under Royal Navy protection. Southerners, typified by Thomas Jefferson, argued instead for a small coastal defense force, on the logic that navies were enormously expensive and tended to reinforce government power at home and get into scrapes abroad. With the Naval Act of 1794, however, the die was cast: the United States would have an oceangoing Navy, and the *United States* and her sister frigates—larger and more powerful than the ordinary frigates of other navies—would show the world that the new nation and its new ships were not to be ignored. Like Decatur, these ships would punch well above their weight, and Decatur's own story would be linked with several of them, including *United States*, *Constitution*, and *Chesapeake*.

After helping to supervise construction of the *United States*, Decatur was determined to sail with her. The frigate launched in May of 1797 under the command of Commodore John Barry, a naval hero of the Revolution (and namesake of my own first destroyer command), and Decatur was formally commissioned as a midshipman in her company in April 1798. Two of his defining traits were instantly apparent: his skill as a sailor and his popularity with his shipmates, from the most senior to the youngest sailors. Under the tutelage of a former Royal Navy officer hired by his father to teach him the principles of seamanship, as well as Barry's practical example, Decatur flourished as a young officer and won the affections not only of his commander but also a lieutenant named James Barron. In today's parlance, we would say he had high "emotional intelligence," meaning people gravitated to him and he was able to understand their character and ingratiate himself with them in positive ways—that is, he was a charismatic leader of the first degree.

In 1799, Decatur was promoted to lieutenant and was baptized by fire into the "honor culture" of his day. While Decatur made the rounds of the Philadelphia dockyards to enlist a crew for the *United States'* next voyage, a merchant sailor roughly insulted the Navy generally and Decatur personally. Decatur seethed but held his tongue and the incident did not escalate—until he reported it to his father. Stephen Sr. insisted that his son defend the honor of his own name, his family, and his service, and Stephen Jr. sent word demanding either an apology or a duel. His antagonist chose pistols, and Decatur—an expert shot—determined to wound him in the hip and did so. This settled the question of honor without loss of life, but also established the already supremely self-confident Decatur as a man just as ready to prove his mettle against pistol fire on land as against cannon fire at sea.

No matter his physical courage and skill, however, the greatest danger to any US naval officer's career in 1800 was the end of the Quasi-War with revolutionary France. After two years of undeclared and little-remembered conflict with ships of France's new republic (to which the US government refused to pay debts incurred to the deposed French monarchy during the American Revolution), the end of hostilities brought back the old anti-naval sentiment—and a mass discharge of officers and sailors. Decatur was among the comparatively tiny group retained on active duty, which put him in a prime position to respond when the Navy was subsequently called upon to settle the longest-running threat to merchant shipping from American shores—North African pirates.

Piracy—especially from the so-called Barbary Coast of North Africa—had been the scourge of the Mediterranean for centuries. As ever, the real purpose of piracy was to make money, and the rulers of the Barbary States were just as happy to take sure profits in tribute as to extract them the hard way on the high seas. Before the Revolution, American ships had been protected by the annual tribute paid by the British, but independence required new arrangements. Without a navy to subdue the pirates, the United States first followed the European custom of paying annual tributes. But it did not take long for patience to wear thin with repeated humiliations and demands for more tribute. Tensions finally boiled over in May 1801, when President Jefferson— ironically previously the staunchest of anti-navalists and anti-interventionists—declared war on the Barbary States and dispatched the Navy to reduce the threat once and for all.

As one of the few officers still holding an active commission when the Navy was suddenly pressed back into service, Decatur sailed with the first US squadron dispatched to the Mediterranean. Still a lieutenant, he served aboard USS *Essex* under the command of William Bainbridge. They crossed the Atlantic in a month and, in the way of nineteenth-century communications, found upon calling at Gibraltar that Tripoli had reciprocally declared war on the United States. Despite the formal state of hostilities, the tiny US squadron could neither bottle up all the pirate state's ships nor immediately take the fight to their extremely well-defended harbors. (Had such a simple solution existed, the larger European navies would have applied it long before.) For the rest of 1801 and most of 1802, Decatur continued cruising aboard *Essex*, then transferred to USS *New York* under the now commodore James Barron, until another dispute of honor ashore—with a Royal Navy officer in Malta, while *New York* was refitting after a weeklong gale at sea—resulted in Decatur being sent back to the United States.

The timing turned out to be fortuitous. Almost as soon as he set foot ashore in his home country, Decatur was sent back to the Mediterranean in command of the small and newly built USS *Argus*, with orders to hand it off to a senior officer in Gibraltar. That done, he took command of the somewhat larger USS *Enterprise* and formed up with the frigate USS *Constitution*. On December 23, 1803, *Constitution* and *Enterprise* overtook a small ship flying the Ottoman flag and carrying Tripolitan soldiers. Decatur and *Enterprise* quickly overpowered the Tripolitans and brought the captured ship as a prize to Syracuse, Sicily, where she was rechristened as USS *Intrepid*. This little ship bearing a big new name would bring Decatur and the US Navy lasting international renown.

Events had been set in train two months earlier when Decatur's former commander, William Bainbridge, had run the *Philadelphia* aground on an uncharted shoal near the mouth of Tripoli harbor. The powerful frigate and symbol of US naval ambition was quickly captured and refloated by the Tripolitans while Bainbridge and his men were pushed into a long and torturous captivity of forced labor. Both tactically and as a matter of pride, it was unacceptable for the *Philadelphia* to be keeping the US Navy out of the harbor rather than keeping the Tripolitans in check. US officers throughout the Mediterranean began scheming ways to get the ship back.

Knowing that there was no sense in pursuing a simple cannon duel between the US squadron and the captured *Philadelphia* backed by all the guns emplaced around the harbor, Decatur put forward a plan based on outwitting rather than overpowering the enemy. He proposed to Commodore Edward Preble, commander of US naval forces in the Mediterranean, to sneak into Tripoli harbor with a hand-picked crew of sailors—at night, in disguise, and under a false flag. Once in the harbor, they would talk their way aboard the *Philadelphia*, surprise the enemy crew, and then either sail the recaptured ship as a "fire ship" at the pirate ships or simply burn her at her moorings. For daring, tactical acumen, and personal risk, Decatur's plan was noteworthy, even in that age of bold action. In terms of providing personal glory if it succeeded, or perhaps even if it failed spectacularly, it was equally remarkable. On January 31, 1804, Preble gave Decatur his approval, ordering the latter to "enter the harbor in the night, board and set fire to the *Philadelphia*."[3] At the time, although an experienced seagoing officer, Decatur was only a twenty-five-year-old lieutenant.

It took two weeks for Decatur to assemble and outfit his all-volunteer crew of eighty Marines, sailors, and a local harbor pilot, and then to sail the *Intrepid* to the point of attack, accompanied by the somewhat larger USS *Syren*. By the evening of February 16, all was finally ready. Dressed in a motley approximation of the garb of local merchant sailors, Decatur and twenty of his boarding party manned the topside of the ship. The rest of the force, consisting of sixty or so Marines and sailors, slipped below *Intrepid*'s deck to hide in groups corresponding to sections of the *Philadelphia*. Decatur hoisted British colors to further increase the deception. By 7:00 p.m., *Intrepid* began making her way into Tripoli harbor, moving in the general direction of *Philadelphia*, while the *Syren* remained just outside the mouth of the harbor as backup.

At this point in his decision-making process, Decatur realized that the die was cast, barring some unlucky setback. His mind would have been turning rapidly over the possible permutations of what lay ahead. Having led boarding parties myself as a junior officer, I can attest to the keen sense of responsibility an officer feels for sailors under his or her command. By 8:00 p.m., an hour into the slow approach, Decatur had ordered silence about the decks. Every thirty minutes, he walked the length of his small command, peering into the dark night, lit by the thin sliver of waxing crescent moon. As 9:00 p.m. approached, he went below for a whispered conversation with the leaders of each of the boarding parties, returning topside to survey the hulk of *Philadelphia* coming closer and closer still. His hope at this point was to take control of the much larger warship and somehow get it sufficiently manned to sail to sea. If not, he would burn it.

The clock in his head kept ticking as he checked the time on the ornate pocket watch he carried. But progress was exceedingly slow: it took two and a half hours for the *Intrepid* to drift to within hailing distance of the *Philadelphia*. By 9:30 p.m., you can imagine the sweat and the stress of the men belowdecks during this excruciating passage, but no one was under any illusions as to the risks if there was suspicion and discovery. It would not have required even a full broadside from the big guns of the *Philadelphia* to utterly destroy the *Intrepid* as she inched her way as innocently as possible across the dark waters of the harbor. The slower her progress, the less threatening the *Intrepid* appeared, and the more thickly fell the curtain of night.

At last, by 9:45 p.m., *Philadelphia* was in hailing distance. The *Intrepid*'s Arabic-speaking Sicilian pilot unfolded his cover story to the Tripolitan sailors on *Philadelphia*'s decks: he was a merchantman battered by a storm in the Mediterranean and forced into Tripoli for repairs, claimed the pilot; having lost his anchors at sea, could he possibly tie up to this big ship overnight? Failing to see an ulterior motive—or perhaps swayed by the universal imperative among sailors to aid brethren in distress—the Tripolitans agreed. Just before 10:00 p.m., *Intrepid* gently bumped alongside the hulking frigate, lines were passed over the rails, and the two ships were lashed together.

Decatur at this point must have felt his heart sink just a bit. It would have been clear as the ships touched their sides that *Philadelphia* was in no condition to sail: her masts were disassembled, and the sails were not visible. For Decatur, like many decision-makers in combat, this moment at 10:00 p.m. crystallized his course of action—he must strike hard, take control, and destroy the ship.

Before anyone on the *Philadelphia* had a chance to reconsider their hospitality, Decatur sprung the trap at just after 10:00 p.m. The Tripolitans, who had ambushed many a sailor under a false flag or feigned surrender, were themselves surprised by a sudden order shouted in English: "Board!" Marines and sailors burst out of the hatches and swarmed onto the *Philadelphia*'s decks, slashing and stabbing with swords and pikes. Decatur had strictly forbidden the use of firearms except in direst need, hoping to maintain the element of surprise aboard ship and in the harbor for as long as he could. The plan unfolded without a hitch and with barely a scratch: within ten minutes the Americans had secured all their assigned sectors of the ship and suffered only one relatively minor sword cut as they killed about twenty Tripolitans. The rest of the startled defenders jumped into the harbor to swim for safety.

This was the moment of maximum tension for the young lieutenant Decatur. By this point, he knew there was no chance to sail, but also that the harbor authorities would be alerted within moments and the city would raise a general alarm. In combat, decisions are often forced down a certain path as options foreclose. This can actually crystallize choices for leaders, and I can picture the entire boarding party turning to Decatur for orders. So often, this is where leaders rise or fall in crisis. The best square their shoulders, speak in a steady and calm voice, and provide crisp direction. By 10:45 p.m., that was precisely what Lieutenant Stephen Decatur did, at the moment of maximum danger. It is also the moment when so many leaders, some of them very good in other less risky scenarios, lose their nerve and decide to withdraw to safety.

With *Philadelphia* secure, Decatur had to undertake the trickiest part of the operation: set a fire certain to destroy the ship, and then escape the burning wreck and the Tripolitan cannons ashore—whose crews would surely respond to the beacon in the harbor. Decatur and his men quickly and carefully made their way about the ship, setting fires throughout while respecting the stores of powder and loaded guns.

This would have taken perhaps fifteen minutes, bringing the clock to roughly 11:00 p.m. As the flames began to spread, the onshore cannons began to speak, yet Decatur remained aboard the *Philadelphia* until flames climbed into the rigging and he was positive the fire would destroy her. With all his raiders and one gravely wounded Tripolitan captive back aboard the *Intrepid*, Decatur finally swung over the rail and made all sail for the open sea. It was not quite 11:30 p.m.

Behind him, *Philadelphia* burned away from her moorings and began to drift back toward the Tripolitan ruler's palace, and her loaded guns fired blindly into the city and across the harbor as their barrels heated up and set off their charges. Still more cannonballs flew overhead in both directions as the Tripolitan artillery fired at the conflagration and the *Syren* waited from outside the harbor to cover *Intrepid*'s escape; miraculously, only one shot actually touched the *Intrepid*, passing harmlessly through one of her sails as she scudded safely out to sea. In less than ninety minutes, from the time he gave the order to board to the time the *Intrepid* sailed clear of the spectacularly burning *Philadelphia*, Lieutenant Decatur had made himself immortal in the annals of naval history at barely twenty-five years of age.

It is hard to imagine the elation Stephen Decatur felt as his small warship cleared the harbor and entered an open seaway. Yet even at this moment, as a decision-maker, his mind would have continued to evaluate the outcome (superb) and measure the risk of an unexpected setback even at this point (being overtaken by a pursuing vessel, or damage to the ship of which he wasn't aware). He would have personally and quickly inspected the ship for seaworthiness, reassured himself of the safety and health of his crew of sailors and Marines, and focused on the navigation of the vessel. Sometimes it is the crisis point that is the most uncomfortable, but the immediate aftermath that is the most dangerous—because you can be tempted to let down your guard. Decatur did not, and by midnight, he could feel reasonably sure it would be a fully successful outcome.

After escaping Tripoli harbor, Decatur made for Syracuse, where he was feted by countrymen, locals, and sometime rivals alike. The pope praised him for striking such a blow against the Islamic pirates; British naval hero Vice Admiral Nelson, who had already smashed a Napoleonic fleet in a risky night action off the coast of Egypt, is reported to have called Decatur's mission "the most bold and daring act of the age." Decatur's commanders wrote to President Jefferson to recommend him for early promotion to captain; the appointment was confirmed retroactive to the date of the raid on February 16, and Decatur to this day is still the youngest person ever to attain that rank in the US Navy, at twenty-five years. As a small point of comparison, I was se-lected quite early for captain—at the age of forty.

Unfortunately, the letter confirming Decatur to cap-taincy arrived in August, in the midst of another battle with Tripolitan pirates that claimed the life of his younger brother, James. Once again, Decatur quickly rounded up a small band of volunteers, identified and boarded the ship of his brother's killer, and routed the pirates in furious hand-to-hand combat. Decatur personally killed the enormous pirate captain and narrowly escaped death himself when one of his crewmen, already wounded, leapt into the way of a saber blow aimed at Decatur's head. Spared at the ex-pense of his shipmate, Decatur dispatched his assailant with a pistol shot.

The remaining sixteen years of Decatur's life and service were similarly filled with honor, glory, and—frequently—pistol fire. After returning to the United States following the first Barbary War, he married Susan Wheeler in 1806. Susan was the daughter of the mayor of Norfolk, Virginia, and al-ready a person of high social standing in her own right; in their fourteen (childless) years of marriage, she and Stephen would establish themselves at the very heart of Washington society. (Their home, Decatur House, still stands directly across the street from the White House and is used by secretaries of the Navy and other prominent government figures for official entertaining to this day.)

Sadly, the seeds of revenge that would eventually sprout into the duel that claimed Decatur's life were planted just one year after his and Susan's marriage. On June 22, 1807, Decatur's old companion and then good friend Commodore James Barron sailed as a passenger aboard the frigate USS *Chesapeake* to take command of US naval forces in the Mediterranean. Barron had hardly gotten out to sea when he found himself under attack from the HMS *Leopard*, a British ship whose commander had formally alleged while still in port that several of his sailors were illegally serving aboard the *Chesapeake*. (This sort of dispute was common in the years leading up to the War of 1812 as the British tried every sort of inducement, violence, and bluffing to keep their ships crewed.) With his decks littered with dead and wounded men and his guns still stowed, Barron struck his colors without firing a shot. When word of the engagement reached the Navy Department, it caused a scandal—and no one was more incensed than Decatur. Barron was court-martialed and found guilty of unpreparedness; Decatur not only sat on the court and voted to convict him but kept up a loud public critique for years afterward. Barron was barred from command for five years and decamped to Denmark with his family to escape the furor and seek employment in the merchant service.

When war broke out with Great Britain again in 1812, Decatur commanded the frigate USS *United States* with great distinction, famously capturing the HMS *Macedonian*. Later in the war, Decatur himself was captured off of New York after being surrounded by and surrendering to a British squadron. In those days, surrendering a ship was an accepted practice among gentlemen—but honor required that surrender happen in the face of stiff odds and generally after putting up a worthy resistance. The *Chesapeake-Leopard* Affair, as it came to be known, was a scandal because Barron had been caught unprepared and could not resist; Decatur, facing certain destruction if he fought on against four enemy frigates, had his sword returned by his British captors in recognition of gallantry in defeat.

After the War of 1812, the United States turned its attention back to the recurring problem of piracy, and Decatur sailed back to the Mediterranean for the Second Barbary War. As commodore of the Mediterranean squadron—the largest fleet put to sea by the United States up to that time—he compelled first the Dey of Algiers and then the rulers of both Tunis and Tripoli to sign terms of peace once and for all, thus removing the perennial scourge of piracy from the Mediterranean. His personal reputation was a critical part of inducing the Arabs to come to the peace table and negotiate.

Decatur once again returned in glory from the Barbary Coast to Washington, DC—this time, having achieved lasting peace without firing a shot. He was soon appointed to serve on the Board of Navy Commissioners and served in that role from 1816 until his death in 1820. In that year, Captain James Barron—who had returned from self-imposed exile in Denmark hungry for a new command and to clear his name—challenged Decatur to a duel as a result of their long-simmering dispute over Barron's conduct aboard the *Chesapeake*. Returning to active duty as the Navy was going through another postwar downsizing, Barron would need all the help he could get to receive another command; Decatur, as a navy commissioner, remained publicly opposed to Barron's further service and was in a position to prevent it. Determined to restore his career (and his income), Barron demanded satisfaction.

The opponents met on March 22, 1820, at the infamous Bladensburg dueling grounds just northeast of Washington, DC. Decatur's second was William Bainbridge, who had grounded the *Philadelphia* on the shoal at Tripoli. In a tragically ironic twist of fate, Bainbridge also harbored some envy for the younger Decatur's success, and may have arranged the unusually dangerous terms of the duel out of spite. Rather than pacing away from each other for fifteen or more paces and then turning to fire as was common, Decatur and Barron began facing each other at a distance of only eight paces. Both fired immediately upon the signal, and both bullets struck home. Barron was badly wounded but survived; Decatur was mortally wounded in the pelvic region. Decatur was carried home alive and a surgeon was called, but nothing could be done to save him. He died in excruciating pain that evening. Although it was too late for Decatur, this pointless loss of a hero did much to finally convince the Navy to clamp down on dueling culture with a formal ban and increasingly rigorous enforcement.

Despite Decatur's untimely death, his legacy lives on in today's Navy—and his raid into Tripoli harbor continues to offer instruction as not merely a supremely daring act of that age but also as an inspiration to bold action in any time and place. In reviewing his decision to steal into the harbor at night—in disguise and at enormous personal risk, where a single mistake could have meant instant destruction under the Tripolitan guns—modern decision-makers need to see both Decatur's personality and his rationale in the context of his times.

To understand Decatur and the trajectory of his life, you have to begin with the burning of *Philadelphia* and his comportment and decision-making skills under extreme duress. Begin with the audacity of the plan—think for a moment about the extreme level of personal risk it entailed. He knew throughout the long, slow approach on the target that any discovery would mean annihilation by the massive guns covering his much smaller ship. Even if they ran that gauntlet, the actual hand-to-hand combat would be deadly, and Decatur knew that his personal presence on the very front line of the assault would be crucial. To even conceive of such a plan—with such a high level of personal risk—is quite extraordinary. But to Stephen Decatur, that was only the opening act.

Once he convinced his chain of command of his highly risky and dangerous plan, he had to handpick a crew, inspect all their weapons, brief them as a group and then many of them (boarding party leaders) individually, practice the maneuver, carefully attend to the sailing qualities of his vessel, lay out a navigational course, ensure everyone was well-fed and primed for combat, and get them into the ship and underway. All of that would have required being awake for most of a thirty-six-hour period, even as he would have encouraged the men under his command to try to get some rest, along with a good meal.

But it is his actions on the scene that truly stand out. As he crawled across the sea miles and entered the harbor for the agonizingly slow approach on *Philadelphia*, Decatur had to continuously play the loop of the operation in his mind. I've done that many times, in a wide variety of operational circumstances, and it is like standing in the middle of a kaleidoscope that is shifting each time you spin the outer cylinder—the decision-maker has to adjust as the circumstances in front of him or her change. Decatur, in the burning of *Philadelphia* and other important moments in his meteoric career, had that ability.

Partly it is inherent, innate to men and women of confidence, something burned into their DNA and enhanced by their upbringing; partly it is the result of training, experience, and reflection. Of all the sailors in this book, Decatur possessed the greatest measure of pure audacity, a quality instilled by a seagoing family, enhanced by his physical stamina and charismatic appearance, and increased over the years by the ways he tested himself in combat (and, sadly, on the field of chance). But it all began in earnest in those charmed and furious ninety minutes in the dark and calm harbor in North Africa, an episode that resonates throughout the twenty-first-century Navy as surely as it did our predecessors in the early nineteenth century.

One additional important piece of context for Decatur's

personality worth noting was the character of the nascent US Navy in which he served. Benjamin Stoddert, the first secretary of the Navy, insisted from the outset that the infant US Navy should make up in attitude what it lacked in size; as he wrote to President John Adams: "Our Navy at this time when its Character is to form, ought to be Commanded by Men who, not satisfied with escaping censure, will be unhappy if they do not receive, and merit praise."[4] Decatur was an exemplar in and of this culture, and Stoddert's assertion has been borne out in Decatur's continued influence on the character of today's Navy. With so many battles to fight in Decatur's day, the way to win praise was to excel in them—and his early and consistent excellence earned praise well beyond his lifetime. Given that praise-seeking culture, it is easy to see why a naturally daring person like Decatur would propose to lead a high-risk, high-reward operation like the raid on Tripoli harbor. He would surely have realized that such a gamble could ensure his fame and honor—which, as dueling culture so bloodily demonstrated, were to be valued above life itself.

But the overarching message to take away from Decatur's life and service is the way he harnessed his daring and ambition to a genuine set of priorities and values that we can still celebrate today. After all, it is not hard to find ambitious twenty-five-year-olds willing to run great risks in pursuit of praise, but few of them go on to lasting fame. In addition to being a matter of personal glory and national honor, the *Philadelphia* raid was also strategically and tactically important: it prevented the Tripolitans from using a large and powerful (captured) asset against the Americans on a mission to defeat them. Given the well-known strength of the harbor's defenses, the subterfuge of a disguised night raid was probably a better bet than risking several capital ships in a daylight assault. And, in retrospect, it fit a pattern in Decatur's life of choosing boldly in service of a greater cause. When he married Susan, Decatur was up-front about his intention to stay in the service rather than "cashing out," as we would say today, on the strength of his early fame; later, during their time as Washington socialites, Decatur offered a famous toast summing up his philosophy: "Our country— in her intercourse with foreign nations, may she always be in the right, and always successful, right or wrong."[5]

Stephen Decatur always liked his chances, and his lifelong appetite for risk earned him a captaincy at age twenty-five, a Congressional Gold Medal, and high praise from Vice Admiral Lord Nelson himself. And yet, given his untimely and much-mourned end, it is also worth drawing a cautionary lesson from his character. No one has ever been always in the right and always successful, and points of pride have tripped up many talented and ambitious people, ending many glittering careers. Even if we can ascribe Decatur's decision to accept Barron's challenge to the honor culture of their times, for example, the decision to fight the duel face-to-face at eight paces was frankly foolhardy. Unlike the *Philadelphia* mission, for which he gained his superior's endorsement and enlisted dozens of volunteers, the duel happened outside not only good sense but also the law and the express wishes of a Navy Department exasperated by the consistent loss of good officers to the fields of chance.

The lessons of Stephen Decatur's life and career still resonate strongly with our naval service today, much as Lord Nelson's character lives on in the approach of the British Royal Navy. First and most obviously, his physical courage was central to how he lived his life. Whether on a cutting-out expedition or lifting a dueling pistol, he was brave and steady under fire. That ethos threads through subsequent commanders and sailors from Farragut to Dewey to Dorie Miller to our warriors at sea today. Second, it would be easy to say that Decatur was too swayed by the chance for glory and therefore took unacceptable levels of risk. But I would say that, overall, he generally found the balance. While he did accept high levels of risk in his decision-making, it was most often balanced by rock-solid planning (as during the *Philadelphia* mission) and—at times—an effort to reduce risks to his crew. Third, Decatur's approach was one of resolute adherence to the value set of his institution. He recognized that in his Navy it was necessary to bravely fight the ship, and if one failed in that primal mission set, there had to be a significant consequence. Hence his harsh approach to a former friend and fellow sea captain, James Barron—which ultimately instigated the chain of events leading to his death.

Physical courage under intense pressure, a balanced and thoughtful approach to risk-taking when time and circumstance permit, and a willingness to accept and impose accountability both for victory and defeat: those three qualities are indeed a fine legacy passed from Decatur to the US Navy. It is one our sailors seek to live up to in this demanding time, often with success and occasionally with failure. In the course of my own career, I tried to follow those fundamental rules of decision-making, especially as I became more senior and recognized my actions would stand as an example to so many under my command. I often thought of Decatur and his bravery, for example, when I traveled Afghanistan and met with our NATO troops there. What struck me then, when I was in my midfifties, was how young and forthright our soldiers, Marines, sailors, and airmen are today. And despite the two centuries of time and the constant changes in our society, I still saw the audacity of a Decatur in their faces again and again. My job, as a vastly senior officer, was to temper that keen sense of personal bravery and focus the chain of command on the need for the balance of planning and the grounding in the higher values of the institution that must be observed and enforced.

Stephen Decatur's meteoric life is a deeply ingrained part of our nation's Navy today. And I believe his example echoes well beyond the Navy and is woven into the risk-taking culture of the nation in so many ways, from Silicon Valley to professional sports. His life's lessons remain important for any decision-maker seeking to find the right balance in the most complex and pressure-packed endeavors.

CHAPTER THREE

Risky Business

———◆———

Rear Admiral David Farragut,
United States Navy

Commander, USS Hartford *and the Seventeen-*
Vessel US Naval Gulf Blockading Squadron

BATTLE OF MOBILE BAY

AUGUST 5, 1864

Damn the torpedoes! Four bells!
Captain Drayton, go ahead! Jouett, full speed!*

———

* Usually paraphrased as "Damn the torpedoes, full speed ahead!"

In the hot summer of 1985, the Navy ordered me to move to Pascagoula, Mississippi. My new set of orders were to become the operations officer of a brand-new *Ticonderoga*-class guided missile cruiser, USS *Valley Forge*. The ship was being built at Ingalls Shipbuilding, which is located on the Gulf Coast roughly between New Orleans, Louisiana, and Mobile, Alabama. I wasn't particularly happy with the location of the building yard. This was not a part of the country I'd ever visited, and my job was complicated by the division of our four-hundred-person crew between San Diego, California (our ultimate home port), and Pascagoula. But my wife, Laura, and I gamely figured out how to split our time between the two locations, renting an apartment in Ocean Springs, Mississippi, not far from the shipyard, and moved in.

Suffice to say, Pascagoula in those days was not one of the

literary hubs of our nation. Very nice people, excellent shrimp restaurants, cold beer, and lots of beautiful beaches for sure—but bookstores and libraries, not so much. This became a problem over time for me, because one thing I had come to enjoy profoundly every week in those halcyon days before the internet was reading the Sunday *New York Times*. At my previous duty station in Boston, where I completed a PhD at the Fletcher School of Law and Diplomacy, it was easy to find the *NYT*. I looked everywhere in the Pascagoula region with no luck. So I called the *Times*, got the subscription desk on the line, and asked for the nearest place I could buy the paper. With an odd kind of pride in her voice, the operator said, "The *New York Times* is not available in the state of Mississippi." Pause. Then she said, "The closest vendor to your location is the newsstand at the Mobile airport in Alabama." So every Sunday morning, I would drive over an hour each way to buy a copy of the *New York Times*.

Besides burning up a fair amount of gas, these trips gradually gave me an appreciation for Mobile, Alabama. It is a lively, culturally attuned city of around two hundred thousand with a vibrant history. Laura and I had many nice afternoons and evenings there at restaurants and bars overlooking the wide and beautiful bay. As we got to know the city better over those long months on the Gulf Coast, I started to learn more about the history of the city—especially about the Civil War's Battle of Mobile Bay. And all of that led me to David Glasgow Farragut, one of the great fighting admirals in the history of the US Navy, and someone whose tolerance for risk was perhaps greater than any of the other decision-makers in this volume.

The more I learned about him, the more intrigued I became with his personal history, loyalty to the Union, and successful naval career. A foster child who went on to be the first rear admiral, vice admiral, and full admiral in the US Navy, he served on every coast of the United States, from Norfolk to the Gulf to California. Farragut fought again and again for the United States and earned every stripe he added to his sleeves over a career of almost sixty years.

His actions in Mobile Bay remain legendary. By 1864, Mobile was the last major port the Confederacy held on the entire Gulf Coast and was therefore of high strategic value. The Confederates had heavily mined the bay with tethered charges that could easily sink a ship after contacting its hull. These devastating devices are better known as "mines" today but were called "torpedoes" then for their long cylindrical shape. After Farragut ordered his flotilla to charge into the bay, one of his ironclads, USS *Tecumseh*, struck one of these torpedoes and sank. While the rest of his captains hesitated or began to withdraw, Farragut made the decision that has caused him to live on in legend.

From the topmast of his flagship, USS *Hartford*, he used a speaking trumpet to query the reason for the delay. After being told it was torpedoes, he said, "Damn the torpedoes!" and ordered the ships to full speed. Farragut guessed that the mines would be too waterlogged from long submersion to function—but a wrong guess or a wrong move could quickly send his ships to the bottom. He chose to simply charge on anyway, and seemingly without a shred of hesitation. In the event, the bulk of his forces made it into the bay and defeated the Confederate forces ashore and afloat, notably beating the well-managed combined forces of Confederate rear admiral Franklin Buchanan, a clever and skillful opponent.

Was it a foolhardy call that turned out lucky? Or a calculation built upon the events of his significant combat experience in the Mexican-American War, piracy in the West Indies, and the War of 1812? A son of the sailing Navy, how much did his knowledge and attitude toward the new technologies of ironclads, mines, and rifled cannon play into his decision? Did the presence of land forces dependent on his success come into his calculus? Farragut made a hard choice, and it turned out to be spectacularly successful, leading to his promotion in December 1864 as the first vice admiral and, a year and a half later, the first full admiral in US history—a rank he held until his death. He would go on to be a pallbearer for Abraham Lincoln, open shipyards on the West Coast after the war, and command the US European Squadron. As we say in the Navy, much success followed his flag. Was it the result of a lucky decision made in the heat of battle, or a carefully calculated hard choice?

Command at sea has always involved living, deciding, and sometimes dying with the caprices of the ever-shifting ocean. In Farragut's day, many careers started at what we would now consider shockingly early ages, and his own was no exception. But Farragut's own exposure to seafaring, death, and transition began even earlier than most. The future hero of the Union was born James Farragut on July 5, 1801, not far from Knoxville, Tennessee. His father, Jordi (known as George), was a Spaniard who had sailed in the American Navy during the Revolution and settled with his wife, Elizabeth, in Tennessee after the war. Four-year-old James sailed for the first time in 1805 when he journeyed with his mother and siblings to join George at his new posting in New Orleans.

This voyage dramatically changed the course of the entire Farragut family's lives. On June 22, 1808, death visited the Farragut household twice. George's friend David Porter Sr., another naval veteran of the Revolution who had been staying with the Farragut family while convalescing from sunstroke and tuberculosis, was first to go. Elizabeth succumbed to yellow fever that same afternoon—leaving young James and his siblings alone with their overwhelmed father. George immediately sought other families to care for his children, and David Porter's son David Jr. offered to take James. Everyone agreed to this arrangement, and Farragut was welcomed into the nucleus of a family that would go on to produce two commodores (David Porter Sr. and his son William) and the first two admirals of the US Navy (David Dixon Porter and Farragut—who took his adoptive father's first name, David, dropping the name James that he had been given at birth).

But in 1808, all those gilded stars that would one day land on their naval collars were yet to come. Farragut had already expressed interest in joining the Navy but had not yet reached the minimum age of ten years for a midshipman's berth. Ultimately, Farragut was able to get a slight head start: he was appointed a midshipman at the tender age of nine and a half. Young as he was, this is also when we begin to see Farragut as he is remembered today: not only in naval uniform but bearing his adoptive father's first name and rapidly taking on the responsibilities of naval leadership under the latter's command.

The War of 1812 broke out just as Farragut was properly getting his sea legs. Sailing aboard USS *Essex* with Porter, he got his first tastes of both combat and command before reaching his teen years. *Essex* captured a number of British warships and whalers, and Porter placed Midshipman Farragut in command of a prize in the summer of 1813. Farragut brought the prize safely into port but was to find the shoe on the other foot in the following year. He was back aboard the *Essex* when, in 1814, the ship attempted to sortie out of Valparaíso, Chile, and was dismasted and captured by two British men-of-war. Farragut himself was wounded in the battle.

During and after the war, Farragut found himself on the expanding perimeter of a growing US global footprint. Sailing under David Porter Jr. aboard the *Essex*, he participated in a star-crossed 1813 landing and subsequent onshore fighting in the Marquesas Islands in the Pacific Ocean. Between the War of 1812 and the Mexican-American War, he spent several cruises on the Mediterranean station and with the so-called Mosquito Fleet in the West Indies—a squadron of small US warships based and tasked with suppressing pirates in the Caribbean. (The Mosquito Fleet might seem insignificant today, but those were the early days of the Monroe Doctrine: Britannia really did rule the waves, and Rear Admiral Alfred Thayer Mahan had not yet come along to make the case for a truly global US Navy. Having just defeated the British again, the United States was only again beginning to project power from beyond its own shores, and pirates—as always—made a convenient target.)

Farragut's career began to accelerate during this time, figuratively cracking on more sail and heading to sea again. Sailing once more under his adoptive father Porter, Farragut was given his first proper command, of the tiny, appropriately named USS *Ferret*. Despite this progression in responsibility, however, Farragut did not advance in rank on time when he failed a preliminary lieutenant's exam in 1821. Happily, Farragut was allowed to remain on duty and in command; after completing his tour in the *Ferret*, he married Susan Marchant in 1823 and was eventually promoted to lieutenant in 1825.

The next two decades, before the Mexican-American War broke out, were professionally quiet but personally rocky. Like so many outstanding wartime commanders, Farragut stagnated somewhat when he could not sail against an enemy. The Navy, too, was drifting. In those still-early days, the perennial question of how to fund the fleet sometimes called its very existence into question. The early 1840s typified Farragut's interwar life: Susan died in 1840, Farragut was made commander in 1841, and he remarried, to a woman named Virginia Loyall, in 1843. But when war broke

out with Mexico in 1846, Farragut sailed south once more—
into the Gulf of Mexico, and into the busiest two decades of
his life.

He began this period as commander of USS *Saratoga*,
sailing the Gulf for almost a year in 1847–48 under the legendary Commodore Matthew Perry (who would go on to
open Japan to the West in 1853). Although the war with
Mexico was a major training ground for Army officers who
would go on to lead on both sides of the Civil War, it was not
as formative for the Navy. Still, wartime operations got
ships out of port and careers back in motion. Farragut did
well in command and continued to attract notice from superiors. In 1853, he was directed by Secretary of the Navy
James Dobbin to establish a new Pacific base for the Navy at
Mare Island, California. Farragut traveled west in 1854 and
spent four years on the project, which proved much more
successful than the earlier experiment in the Marquesas. He
was promoted to captain in 1855 and commissioned the
Mare Island Naval Shipyard in 1858.

With the shipyard well established, Farragut returned
home to Virginia with a weather eye on the political horizon. The clouds of war were gathering once again—within
the United States. Farragut correctly surmised that the outcome would not be peaceful, and he would therefore be required to declare his loyalty and render his services to either

North or South. Outspoken in his commitment to the Union as the crisis deepened, Farragut ultimately moved his family to the outskirts of New York City on the eve of war to prove the point.

Despite this clear signal of his own loyalties, it would require one more intervention from the Porter clan for the Navy to trust Farragut with a major command in the new conflict. David Dixon Porter advocated at the Navy Department on his adoptive brother's behalf and finally helped persuade the department to order Farragut back to command at sea. Farragut took command of his new flagship, the steam schooner USS *Hartford*, in February 1862, and once again set sail for the Gulf of Mexico. Although the ships under his command were once again formally known as a blockading squadron, Union strategy made clear that Farragut would not only be cruising the Gulf but actively attacking the mainland—starting with his early hometown of New Orleans.

The Civil War is not widely remembered as a naval conflict. But the Union plan for victory—aptly named Anaconda, after the snake species—was premised on splitting and encircling the South by water in order to gradually strangle it. Picture a two-headed snake: while its steel belly walled off the rebellion from foreign aid and trade, one head would strike down the Mississippi River and the other would force its way up. As the snake squeezed ever tighter, the South would choke on all the cotton it could grow while the industrialized Federal forces crushed the rebels.

Promoted to the nonspecific rank of flag officer (the US Navy still refused to formally create any rank higher than commodore) and in command of the Gulf Blockading Squadron, Farragut drove the southern head of the Anaconda strategy, which called for blockading southern ports and controlling the Mississippi river. And though his titular blockading mission was important and effective, its true objective was the port of New Orleans—the incoming and outgoing terminus of Southern inland shipping, just as it had been for the Spanish and French empires before. As the largest city in the Confederacy and the southern gateway to the Mississippi River, New Orleans was an extremely valuable target for Union attack. Farragut and David Dixon Porter teamed up to lead the assault in fitting solidarity, with Farragut commanding the ships of the line and Porter leading a flotilla of mortar schooners. The ten-day battle began on April 18, 1862, with heavy but ineffectual bombardment of Forts Jackson and St. Philip, which—together with a huge iron chain across the river—guarded the southern approach to the city. After five days of shelling with little to show for it, Farragut determined to simply force his way through. In a prelude to his triumph at Mobile Bay, he weighed the odds and bet on speed and surprise against the forts' formidable but relatively immobile firepower.

Under cover of darkness, Farragut made his move in the early hours of April 24. He ordered his captains to make for a break in the chain across the river and keep sailing as fast as they could even if the forts opened fire. The gambit paid off: although the ships were spotted and fired upon in transit, they kept up their speed while returning fire, and the obscuring smoke and darkness kept the surprised Confederate defenders from sinking any but one of the Union ships as they rushed past. With no defenses farther upriver, the way lay open to New Orleans, which Farragut proceeded to take as the demoralized and stranded Confederate soldiers mutinied in the forts. The victory is hailed as a turning point in the war, and Congress recognized Farragut's success with the newly created rank of rear admiral.

After taking New Orleans, Farragut kept pushing aggressively and mostly successfully up the Mississippi. But he made a costly mistake along the way. In March of 1863, Farragut was supposed to provide the naval punch in a combined attack on the Confederates at Port Hudson, Louisiana, along with land forces under the command of Union general

Nathaniel Banks. Farragut unilaterally decided to press his attack the night before the agreed-upon time of the assault. It is not completely clear whether Farragut tried to inform Banks of the change in timing, but in either case, Banks's troops did not launch their assault simultaneously. Thus unhindered, the Confederates were able to focus on driving Farragut's ships back—and similarly dispatched Banks's eventual attack the following morning.

Farragut spent the next three-plus months sailing up and down the Mississippi interdicting supplies meant for Confederate defenders at Vicksburg. That city finally fell to General Ulysses S. Grant on July 4, 1863, and Port Hudson followed on July 9. With those cities' capitulation, the riverine element of the Anaconda Plan was accomplished. Farragut sailed south, back to the Gulf, and began planning and preparation for the next and greatest fight of his life.

After New Orleans, Mobile was the most important remaining Confederate port on the Gulf. And, with New Orleans back under Union control, it was a major point of entry for the blockade runners that darted out from Havana carrying goods and matériel for the Deep South. The city was naturally well defended by the bay and the barrier islands beyond. Guarding the entrance to the bay, Fort Gaines (twenty-six guns) sat to the west and Fort Morgan (forty-six guns) to the east—plus a novel and ungentlemanly string of submerged mines (as previously explained, then known as "torpedoes") deployed across the western part of the channel. As at New Orleans, victory would require getting past both forts in order to cut them off, and that in turn would require sailing through the minefield and into the teeth of the small but deadly Confederate flotilla beyond.

Sporting or not, the Confederates had placed the mines to counter exactly the kind of ships Farragut commanded. His squadron typified the ongoing transformation in the architecture and conduct of war at sea in the mid-nineteenth century, with seven ships of the line (including his flagship, *Hartford*) made mostly of wood and powered by sail and steam, about twice as many smaller wooden gunboats, and four steam-powered ironclads. This gave Farragut more options than a commander in his position would have had ten or twenty years before, as well as the additional vulnerabilities of the ironclads, which rode low in the water with their crews confined inside—just where the torpedoes were designed to strike.

Farragut's battle plan was designed to deploy all the resources at his disposal to greatest advantage. He paired iron with wood, large with small—and, in a more successful echo of his hurried attack on Port Hudson, soldiers with ships. Typically, he also called for audacity and alacrity. Having learned from his experience at New Orleans, Farragut did not count on reducing the forts by naval bombardment but planned instead to neutralize them by getting past their guns and cutting them off from the city they were meant to protect and upon which they depended for supply. Safety and success would rely on speed and on charging through the minefield unscathed.

Like many great plans, Farragut's was detailed and involved, but fundamentally simple. Since he would be forced to sail directly under the guns of Fort Morgan at close range, he planned to present his strongest side to Fort Morgan while presenting Fort Gaines with its own set of problems. The attack would begin simultaneously on land and at sea, with soldiers landing on Dauphin Island to bombard Fort Gaines while sailors charged through the channel, firing at Fort Morgan from the channel and seaward sides. All depended on coordination and unhesitatingly aggressive execution.

With no plans for an early bombardment, as at New Orleans, Farragut used the days leading up to the battle strictly for preparation and positioning. The countdown began in earnest on August 1 with the arrival of a ship of Union troops commanded by General Gordon Granger. After linking up with Farragut's squadron offshore, the troops landed over the beach on the southern side of Dauphin Island on August 3 and marched on Fort Gaines on August 4. Granger's soldiers spent the evening digging themselves in and preparing an artillery attack to coincide with the naval battle set to kick off the next morning.

Meanwhile, Farragut organized his ships for a strong run around the fort. He put the four ironclads, led by USS *Tecumseh*, on his right, hugging the shoreline and closest to the fort. The seven larger wooden ships, including Farragut's flagship *Hartford*, would stagger somewhat behind and to port of the ironclads, and each would shelter a smaller gunboat lashed to its port side. Far below, outside the bay, he left a small detachment of gunboats to screen the attack from any surprises and distract Fort Morgan's defenders with some shelling. As he constructed his main battle line, Farragut planned to place his own ship first in line but yielded to pressure from his captains to not put himself at such personal risk. Luckily, he conceded only one place in line: sailing second, *Hartford* and Farragut would not be first to risk the guns and mines but would be close enough to see the action before all was obscured by smoke.

The Union guns opened fire on both sides of the channel a few minutes before 7:00 a.m. on the morning of August 5. Granger's soldiers and their artillery attacked and soon overpowered Fort Gaines, securing the western side of the channel; meanwhile, the naval action unfolded almost as swiftly but not nearly as cleanly. As the ships fought northward, rounding Fort Morgan, the billowing smoke from both sides' guns totally obscured Farragut's view of the battle. Unable to move forward in line, the admiral instead moved upward—climbing *Hartford*'s rigging to the mast top in search of a view over the smoke. Seeing this, the *Hartford*'s captain, Percival Drayton, sent a petty officer after the admiral with a piece of line and orders to lash Farragut securely to the mast lest he be flung overboard by a sudden roll of the ship.

Secured above the smoke, Farragut soon had a bigger concern than a sideways lurch: the lead ships of the line were inexplicably slowing down just minutes into the fight and still between the forts. Farragut knew his fleet could not survive long in the jaws of the forts—and that the same smoke that had blocked his view would surely be beckoning the Confederate ships beyond. If the enemy squadron, led by the powerful ironclad ram CSS *Tennessee*, could move quickly enough to seal off the mouth of the bay beyond the minefield, Farragut's fleet would be trapped and likely doomed to die in the channel. It was shortly after dawn on August 5, 1864. The Battle of Mobile Bay was about to unfold in earnest.

At 7:40 a.m., a massive explosion ripped across the water, drowning out even the din of ongoing battle. The lead Union ironclad, *Tecumseh*, had struck a torpedo. She sank in the space of a couple of minutes, taking over one hundred of her crew with her, including her captain. With ships and forts still firing, Farragut ordered a ship's boat out to pick up the few survivors. Glancing up, he saw the *Brooklyn* stop and begin to reverse back toward the squadron already dangerously bunched behind her. Farragut, still lashed to his perch on *Hartford*'s mast and with no way of knowing exactly what was happening aboard *Brooklyn*, saw the loss of not only his plan but probably the battle and possibly his fleet. Farragut had three choices: hang back and wait for *Brooklyn* to resolve or explain the problem or sail around her— straight into the minefield that had just claimed *Tecumseh* in spectacular fashion.

This is a moment that is hard to comprehend even in the context of "routine" combat operations, if such a thing exists. Think of yourself walking into a minefield on land, and literally just a few yards ahead of you, a colleague steps on a mine and is blown to bits in front of your eyes. Safety lies behind you, and the temptation would certainly be to at least pause and assess—except bullets are flying at you from both flanks. The only safe course is simply to back up, readdress the challenges, and formulate a new plan. Most of us would do so—but not Farragut. At this point, he is over sixty years old but remains a vigorous and handsome figure who knows only life at sea and bears a passing resemblance to an older version of the actor Matthew McConaughey. He has seen his share of tight corners, but nothing remotely like the situation he faced in Mobile Bay on that morning.

Farragut's blood was up, and there was no time to ponder the options. At that moment, he was literally bound to the mast of his ship, swaying side to side with every motion of the *Hartford*.

It was just after 8:00 a.m., and once more, Farragut gambled on speed and decisive action—and an educated guess that, despite the *Tecumseh*'s tragic misfortune, most of the mines in the harbor would have corroded beyond use by long immersion in salt water. Down the speaking tube, the admiral barked his now legendary directive, choosing the risky way forward over either an ignominious retreat or almost certain destruction under the forts' guns. His phrasing wasn't precisely recorded, but most sources agree it was some version of this: "Damn the torpedoes! Four bells! Captain Drayton, go ahead! Jouett, full speed!"[1]

Although no one is completely certain what was actually said (or heard) in this moment, there is no doubt that Farragut and *Hartford* surged past *Brooklyn* and into the bay. In any case, "four bells" would indeed have been the signal for "full speed ahead" on *Hartford*'s engine-room telegraph (controlled by Captain Drayton), and James Jouett, in command of the gunboat *Metacomet* lashed to *Hartford*'s port side, would have necessarily had to keep up. *Hartford* and *Metacomet* made it through without setting off any further mines, as did the twelve other wooden ships behind them—including *Brooklyn*, which fell back in as the others sailed past. By around 8:00 a.m., about an hour into the battle, the Union ships were finally beyond the forts and into the bay.

In his fascinating book about the challenges of writing military history, *Damn the Torpedoes*, Brian Burrell points out that the phrase "damn the torpedoes" did not actually appear in any account of the battle until eight years after Farragut's death and thus fourteen years after the battle itself. It does not appear in any official account of the battle.[2] Nonetheless, it has passed into received history and serves as a sort of shorthand for decisions made in the face of grave risk.

As they passed the forts, the larger Union ships cast off their smaller companions to chase down their Confederate counterparts, and at about 8:30 a.m, Farragut ordered the larger ships to anchor. Just as they were preparing to do so, however, the Confederate ironclad ram *Tennessee* raced toward the Union ships in a quixotic solo attack at 8:45 a.m. "I was not long in comprehending his intention to be the destruction of the flagship [*Hartford*]," Farragut wrote in his detailed after-action report. "The monitors [ironclads] and such of the wooden vessels as I thought best adapted for the purpose were immediately ordered to attack the ram, not only with their guns but bows on at full speed, and then began one of the fiercest naval combats on record."[3]

Too well armored to be sunk by wooden foes yet insufficiently armed to sink them, *Tennessee* carried on the fight in the lower bay for the better part of an hour, tracing a backward question mark as she traded cannon fire and ramming runs with the large Union ships. Eventually, two Union ironclads got into the fray, trapping *Tennessee* under fierce Union cannon fire. Still afloat but with armor buckling and her officers and crew decimated by splinters from her interior wooden structure, *Tennessee* finally surrendered at about 10:00 a.m., bringing the naval battle of Mobile Bay to a close. As at New Orleans, the now irrelevant forts and their defenders held out somewhat longer: Fort Gaines formally surrendered on August 8, and Fort Morgan—completely surrounded and bombarded from land and sea—resisted until the morning of August 23, fully two and a half weeks after Farragut forced his way past.

The victory at Mobile Bay was in many ways the apogee of Farragut's long career and certainly enabled the effective success of the maritime portion of the Anaconda strategy. With the Mississippi River and the major Gulf ports under Union control, the South was geographically divided and substantially choked off from supply. The war had less than a year to run, and much of the endgame would now be played out between the armies on land. Victory at Mobile Bay may also have helped President Lincoln's campaign for reelection in the fall of 1864, and Lincoln promoted Farragut to the newly created rank of vice admiral on December 23 of that year. After the war's end, Congress authorized the rank of full (four-star) admiral and conferred that grade on Farragut, making him the US Navy's first admiral on July 25, 1866.* Poignantly, his adoptive brother David Dixon Porter was eventually promoted to the same rank on August 15, 1870—the day after Farragut died.

Farragut held one final postwar command at sea, that of the European Squadron from 1867–68. In recognition of his service to the Union, this officer whose loyalty was initially considered suspect by the Department of the Navy was kept on active duty for the rest of his life. He died in Portsmouth,

---

* Not to be confused with the rank of Admiral of the Navy George Dewey. Farragut was the US Navy's first admiral; Dewey was its first (and only) admiral of the Navy. (Dewey's rank is itself not to be confused with that of Fleet Admiral William "Bull" Halsey. In current practice, Dewey would wear six stars, Halsey five, and Farragut four—but all held the highest naval rank authorized during their times of service, and no US admiral has been conferred more than four stars since 1945.)

New Hampshire, on August 14, 1870, having spent fifty-nine of his sixty-nine years in naval uniform.

Looking back at that career, it would be too simple to conclude that Farragut was only an aggressive or impulsive commander. There is a difference between choosing and acting decisively in the midst of battle and simply throwing caution to the winds or going on pure speculation and hunches—and it would be unwise to lift the phrase "Damn the torpedoes!" completely out of context to justify recklessness. But if we keep his life and actions in perspective, Farragut holds several important lessons for modern decision-makers.

First, Farragut proved adaptable to revolutionary change in the technology and character of his profession. The beginning of his service echoed that of Vice Admiral Lord Nelson's, the most iconic of sailing admirals; by the end of his career, the *Dreadnought* era of steel ships, rifled guns, and submarine threats was just coming into view over the horizon. In a peacetime context of today's world, realize that many senior executives today at big established companies have likewise been witnesses to and participants in an era of great change, from the world of the paper memo to that of fax and the smartphone and on to the now ubiquitous use of video communication. While certainly not an early adopter, Farragut managed to adapt his views of new technologies (like ironclads) as they proved themselves, and to modify their uses to suit his needs (as he did by screening his wooden ships with iron ones at Mobile Bay). Good decision-makers avail themselves of all the advantages that technology can afford them.

Second, Farragut was an extremely powerful example of the value of decisive action based on calculated odds. This worked well for him at New Orleans and especially at Mobile Bay. In his detailed report of the action at Mobile, he explained the conclusions he had drawn about the minefield days before he chose to sail into it at full speed:

> I steamed through between the buoys where the torpedoes were supposed to have been sunk. These buoys had been previously examined by my flag-lieutenant, J. Crittenden Watson, in several nightly reconnaissances [*sic*]. Though he had not been able to discover the sunken torpedoes, yet we had been assured by refugees, deserters, and others of their existence, but believing that from their having been some time in the water, they

were probably innocuous, I determined to take the chance of their explosion.[4]

This meticulous preparation for battle—in reconnaissance, in general orders to his squadron, in coordination with land forces, and above all in his own mind and soul—shows that "Damn the torpedoes!" was not merely a cavalier impulse of the moment. To paraphrase Sun Tzu, Farragut made extensive preparations for victory by careful study beforehand. His decision in the moment was not merely a product of that moment, and this calculating preparation is what distinguishes Farragut as a decision-maker and not merely a lucky swashbuckler. The more a decision-maker sweats the details before going into action, the higher the odds of making successful choices.

Finally, Farragut combined his calculating rational mind and unquestioned physical courage with a genuine personal touch that endeared him to the sailors under his command. Though we remember him today as *the* hero of Mobile Bay, he presents his own decisions and actions matter-of-factly in comparison to those of his sailors. He refers briefly and without a whiff of accusation to seeing "some difficulty ahead" during the battle in *Brooklyn*; as for his own gallantry, he writes: "I determined at once, as I had originally intended, to take the lead, and . . . dashed ahead with the *Hartford*, and the ships followed on, their officers believing that they were going to a noble death with their commander in chief."[5] The report concludes with "warmest commendations" to his officers and men—at length and in many instances by name—"not only for the untiring zeal with which they had prepared their ships for the contest, but for their skill and daring in carrying out my orders during the engagement."[6] No leader of people, no matter how brave, can truly go it alone, and Farragut's reporting style makes clear that he had earned the trust and eager followership of those who served with him. Highlighting his crews' dedicated devotion rather than puffing up his own decisiveness was typical of Farragut and showed that he well understood the importance of organizational execution based on trust earned over time. Having skin in the game not only raises the acuity of a decision-maker but also inspires his teammates.

Mindful adoption of new technologies and techniques, decisive action based on strong preparation and calculated odds, and bravery with a human touch are all qualities demanded and expected of modern decision-makers, and Farragut offers good guidance in all three areas. Looking back on the sheer stubbornness in a close fight of John Paul Jones, and the clever ingenuity in combat of Stephen Decatur, it is easy to see the impact that Farragut had on the still very young US Navy. His decision-making approach was at once technology- and fact-based, but also required a high tolerance for risk.

He was a transition figure between the more elegant age of sail and the coming era of heavy steel ships armed with massive long-range guns. Making decisions in times of transition is perhaps the hardest of métiers—because what is known and accepted as gospel is changing, often at rapid speed. This is especially true when catalyzed with the exigencies of war. This style of decision-making was the beginning of what we might think of as modern analysis in combat settings, and has remained the baseline for US Navy actions. Just as he sailed the cusp dividing the age of sail (John Paul Jones and Stephen Decatur), Farragut created much of what we think of today as the combat decision process of the steel Navy—which as we shall see becomes part of the decision process for other figures in this volume.

As I mentioned in the introduction, when I worked as senior military assistant for Secretary of Defense Donald Rumsfeld three years after 9/11, he would begin every briefing session by insisting on knowing what assumptions the briefer had accepted before commencing the analysis. He was getting at the concept of "known and unknown," as he ultimately titled his memoir of service in the second Bush administration.[7] From a decision-maker like Farragut, we get a sense of how important it is to combine the hard work of analysis with grace under extreme pressure—Ernest Hemingway's description of courage. In my many seagoing assignments, I tried to understand the assumptions that guided the orders from above, maintain a deep understanding of the technology both of my warships and perhaps more importantly of my opponents, prepare deeply for the most important events, and maintain a sense of calm at the most intense moments. I did not always succeed, but I had good models before me, both in Farragut and in Dewey, the subject of the next chapter. I will close with the highest praise I can give any of the figures in this book: Admiral David Farragut was a courageous yet thoughtful decision-maker, and one under whose flag I would gladly sail.

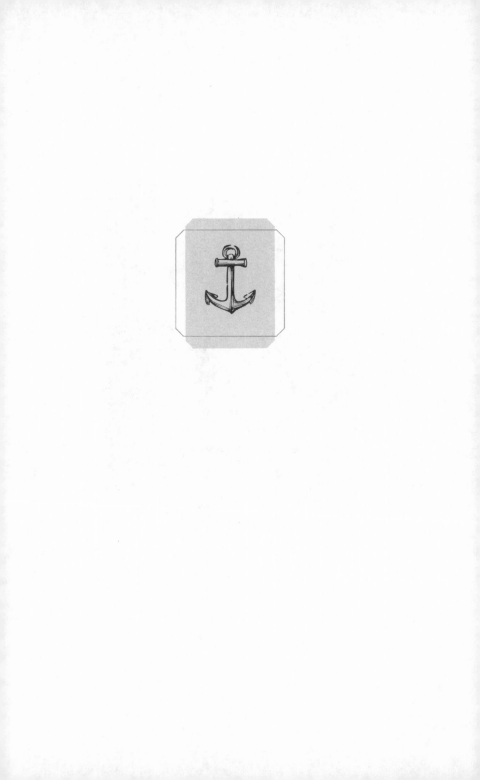

CHAPTER FOUR

Cool Hand George

Commodore George Dewey, United States Navy[1]

Commander, US Asiatic Fleet

BATTLE OF MANILA BAY

MAY 1, 1898

You may fire when ready, Gridley.

In May of 2018, I was asked to give the graduation address at Norwich University in Vermont. At the time, I was the dean of the Fletcher School of Law and Diplomacy and several years into my post-Navy life. I had given several commencement speeches previously and enjoyed the format. The real challenges are keeping the speech short, the students awake, and the faculty mildly interested. Avoiding bromides and platitudes is key (never say things like "reach for the stars," "all you have to do is dream it," or "be kind to others"). Equally important is maintaining humility and a sense of humor. A real plus is having a local hook, something that shows the assembled crowd that you've done your homework and "get" the culture and history of the school.

The oldest private military college in the United States, Norwich University was founded in 1819—before Annapolis, the Citadel, or the Virginia Military Institute. It has more than four thousand students and a vibrant corps of cadets who are commissioned into all the different services. Located in the tiny town of Northfield, Vermont, it is a long way from the sea and predictably has produced a succession of stalwart Army officers (including well over a hundred generals) through its two-hundred-year history. As I began my search for a suitable "hook," I was quite surprised to discover that the highest-ranking person ever to pass through Norwich was not a general but an admiral. And not just any admiral, either, but the only formally designated lifelong admiral of the Navy in American history: George Dewey, victor of the lopsided Battle of Manila Bay in 1898.

Up until that point, I'd had only a passing knowledge of George Dewey as the answer to the Navy trivia question "Who is the highest-ranking officer in the history of the Navy?" And, of course, as a midshipman at Annapolis I had learned the basics of the Battle of Manila Bay where, as commander of the Asiatic Fleet, Dewey calmly ordered his forces into the battle with the simple order to his flag captain, "You may fire when ready, Gridley." But the more I researched the life of this sixty-two-year veteran of the Navy, who began his career fighting in the Civil War and ended his service with an accurate (though controversial) prediction of a coming world war with Germany in the twentieth century, the more I became interested in how he made decisions. In the speech at Norwich, I wanted to make him come alive for the audience and draw some life lessons for the cadets and the rest of the student body.

I began with his immensely readable autobiography, which captures his steady, calm, and resolute voice across the nearly two centuries going back to his birth in 1837. It reads in terms of tone and sobriety much like the classic memoirs of Ulysses S. Grant, felt by many to be the best military memoir in American history. Dewey's volume has that kind of restrained pace and honesty to it and is in a sense a seagoing version of Grant, set in the mid- to late nineteenth century. While he glosses over a few moments in his long career (see the somewhat skeptical *Admiral of the New Empire* by Ronald Spector[2]), overall it reads to me as direct and honest.

In my research, I discovered to my surprise that Dewey was a true hellion in his youth, someone who repeatedly bucked authority, got into serious fistfights, and had several brushes with the law. As a result, his father shipped him off to a military school, thinking it would instill some discipline in this wild child. That school, of course, was Norwich. Though not fully explained in the autobiography, there are reports that he was expelled from Norwich for "drunkenness and herding sheep into the barracks." That experience was apparently not an insurmountable impediment to his subsequent enrollment in the Naval Academy, which also claims him.

In many ways, he was *not* an extraordinary junior or mid-grade officer, although he had some memorable moments on the Mississippi during the Civil War during the days of the extensive blockade that eventually choked off the Southern states. There was a sense of normalcy about him, and few would have predicted he would ascend to the absolute heights of the naval service. For example, in the years between the Civil War and what he called "the Spanish War," he served two years as a lighthouse inspector and four years as naval secretary of the Lighthouse Board.[3] But he was brave, thorough, and—having gotten his temper under control—began to rise steadily if not spectacularly through the ranks. It is important to remember that he was also a deep admirer of Admiral Farragut, and indeed fought under him in several notable Civil War battles on the Mississippi.[4] Yet he continued to have a rough streak that would emerge in certain circumstances. One biographer said he had a "lifelong pattern of striking first and filling out forms later."[5]

By the time he reached flag rank, Dewey had settled himself and earned the friendship (and political influence) of Theodore Roosevelt and several other up-and-comers in Washington. Dewey's appointment to command of the

Asiatic Fleet fulfilled a lifelong dream to lead a squadron in forward operations—and happened just in time to get a call to action against the Spanish colonies in the Pacific. His decision to sail immediately for Manila Bay, stretch his logistic chain to its absolute breaking point, and disregard the possibility of mines in the vast harbor in order to strike hard and fast at the Spanish fleet is worth examining closely.

George Dewey was born on December 26, 1837, in Montpelier, the state capital of Vermont. His mother died when he was only five, so young George developed an early and strong admiration of his father. Julius Dewey was a medical doctor, devout Episcopalian, and well-connected figure in Vermont's political scene. Young George's wild streak manifested in myriad ways. He walked blindfolded down the stairs of the Vermont statehouse on the first day of a legislative session to shock onlookers. He decided to ford a river after a heavy storm just to see if he could do it; in the process, he lost his father's wagon and nearly his own life. Dewey later described his behavior with generous circumspection: "The nature of my disposition led me into a great many adventures. Certainly, I was full of animal spirits, and I liked things to happen wherever I was."[6] Reading between the lines, you can see the plain fact: he was more than a handful.

Dewey was shipped off to Norwich in 1852 but remained for only two years. His rebellious behavior continued. When the bills for private education piled up, the elder Dewey cut his son off from expenses and returned him to Montpelier. George targeted the Naval Academy as his next preferred landing point. The Naval Academy had been founded only nine years earlier; the school was very much still in start-up mode and facing organizational resistance from senior military leadership aligned with the Army (a disagreement that is continually hashed out at the annual Navy-Army football game). George secured a nomination through his father's political connections and the timely decision by the first-in-line candidate to pursue a life in the priesthood instead. As Julius and George Dewey made their way down the East Coast to Annapolis, the elder Dewey directed his son with words that would echo forty-five years later in Manila Bay: "George, I've done all I can for you. The rest you must do for yourself."

George Dewey's time at Annapolis was still marked by emotional outbursts and physical violence. When provoked by his peers, Dewey always gave at least as good as he got. He participated in at least one duel, which was called off only when concerned friends of both parties notified the school authorities. The largest fault line lay between those from the North and South, presaging the outbreak of the Civil War just a few years later. Dewey's fortitude could not be underestimated. Only fifteen of the sixty students who entered in 1854 graduated from the Academy—a 75 percent attrition rate, more than five times the current rate. Dewey graduated fifth in his tiny class.[7]

Dewey's true Navy career began on April 19, 1861, when he was promoted to lieutenant just one week after the shelling of Fort Sumter and the start of the Civil War. He served initially alongside his commander and idol, David Farragut. Indeed, Dewey was an enthusiastic participant in the entirety of Farragut's campaign. He served on the steamship *Mississippi* during the Battle of New Orleans and ably saved a drowning sailor when the ship sank during the Battle of Port Hudson. Dewey was promoted to the executive officer of a ship in Farragut's personal squadron where he developed a deep admiration for Farragut's decisiveness and talent for command. He continued to perform well and was named executive officer of USS *Colorado*.[8]

Dewey's career prospered during the Civil War but stalled once the war was over. Over thirty years would go by between Lee's surrender at Appomattox and Dewey's date with destiny in May 1898. The Navy shrank precipitously after 1865 and the ability to progress quickly up the ranks shrank along with it. Like many Navy officers of that era, the ambitious Dewey struggled with the roles of peacetime. He married Susan B. Goodwin in 1867 while working at the Portsmouth Naval Shipyard in Kittery, Maine, but she tragically died a few days after giving birth to their first child. He taught at the Naval Academy, commanded the hospital ship USS *Supply*, and was a member of the Lighthouse Board based out of New York City. These duties were punctuated by occasional command of warships that never saw combat.

But Dewey preferred any sea duty to his time in Washington, a life that was to him too claustrophobic, political, and full of bureaucracy. He became the chief of the Bureau of Equipment in 1889, responsible for all naval acquisitions as steam power, metal armor, and rifled guns were all becoming the norm. The Navy was trying to catch up technologically to its European peers. But that job lasted for only four years before he returned to the Lighthouse Board. He later returned to Washington as a commodore to head the Board of Inspection and Survey.

Still, Dewey's time in Washington put him on course to Manila, if not necessarily because of what he did but who he knew. Theodore Roosevelt became assistant secretary of the Navy in 1897 while Dewey was on the Board of Inspection and Survey. The future president took a strong liking to Dewey's dynamic personality, no doubt because it reflected

Roosevelt's own bias for action. This partnership came to the fore when the Asiatic Fleet needed a new commander in late 1897. The presumptive favorite, Commodore John Howell, was backed by Rear Admiral Crowninshield, the head of the powerful Bureau of Navigation. Political maneuvering worthy of *Game of Thrones* ensued. Letters from Capitol Hill supporting Howell were already being received by Navy Secretary John Long. Roosevelt convinced Dewey to use any political influence he had on Capitol Hill to secure the nomination. Dewey's deep political connections to Vermont paid off; his senator was able to advocate for Dewey directly to President McKinley and get his approval, doing an end-run around Navy leadership. But that left understandably hard feelings in the Department of the Navy; Secretary Long and Rear Admiral Crowninshield denied Dewey the customary right to become an acting rear admiral while commanding the Asiatic Fleet.

And if the petty politics were not bad enough, Dewey faced an even more difficult politico-military situation in Asia. On the political front, relations between the United States and Spain were deteriorating rapidly. Cuba was still a Spanish colony at the time, riven by sporadic attempted revolts. Meanwhile, the newly outward-looking United States began to see the island as a too-close-for-comfort outpost of a foreign power and helped broker a transitional agreement between Spain and Cuban insurgents in 1895 to lead to independence in 1898. But a new wave of revolutionary violence broke out in 1897, leading to Spanish reprisals and the acrimony with the United States.

On the military front, Dewey was steaming into an uncertain situation on the other side of the world. The Spanish colonial holdings in the Philippines would be in his region. If tasked to fight the Spanish, Dewey would need to do so with a small fleet of ships thousands of miles away from the nearest American supply point. He received little in the way of help from Washington, which he fought viciously to secure as much ammunition and coal as he could. Dewey feared a protracted conflict would leave him without enough material to prosecute operations so far from home. Nor was there much assistance in the way of intelligence. When he took the position, "[a] long official letter transmitting the files and records of the command to its new commander-in-chief was interesting, in that it contained no hint of the pregnant events then impending. Uneasy state of affairs in Korea, some anti-missionary riots in China, the seizure of Kiau Chau Bay by the Germans one month earlier, the attitude of the Japanese, and some minor international matters were mentioned; but in no manner was there any forecast given of the work in which the [Asiatic Fleet] would soon be so vitally interested."[9] When Dewey asked for charts of the Philippines, those he received were twenty years old. The situation was clear: Dewey would essentially be operating alone.

Dewey's decisive character and go-it-alone-if-necessary attitude was perfectly suited for this environment. By January 1898, he had reached Asia and set about pulling his ragtag Asiatic Fleet together, a group that would eventually include six combat ships of varying quality and a stray Coast Guard cutter. By February 11, Dewey saw the deteriorating situation with Spain and, without orders, moved his flagship USS *Olympia* from Japan to Hong Kong. Four days later, USS *Maine* exploded in Havana Harbor. By February 25, the official order came from Washington to move the entire fleet to Hong Kong. Through March and mid-April, the United States and Spain engaged in a diplomatic tit for tat, recalling diplomats and threatening each other with force. By April 21, the United States announced a blockade of Cuba with the goal of ending Spanish presence on the island. War had come. But unlike what jingoistic newspapers of the day would predict, American victory was not assured. Dewey later recounted a story in which British officers in Hong Kong wistfully said goodbye to their American colleagues, assuming they were sailing to their imminent demise in the face of the supposedly impregnable Spanish defenses in the Philippines.

The British governor general of Hong Kong requested that the US Asiatic Fleet leave his jurisdiction on April 24, in keeping with the laws of neutrality. Commodore Dewey was still waiting for his intelligence source in Consul General Oscar F. Williams, so to stall for time, he moved the fleet to Mirs Bay, just east of Hong Kong. He gambled that the central authorities in China were less able than the British in Hong Kong to evict his forces.

By April 25, Dewey received official word from the secretary of the Navy about the outbreak of the war and his new mission: "War has commenced between the United States and Spain. Proceed at once to Philippine Islands. Commence operations particularly against the Spanish fleet. You must capture vessels or destroy. Use utmost endeavor."[10] This was the extent of Dewey's instructions. He was commanding a small fleet, far from any American supply posts, anchored illegally in a neutral country, and told to engage an entrenched force of unknown strength in a very defendable harbor. The fleet remained in Mirs Bay for an agonizing three days before Williams arrived. The ship carrying the consul was sighted in the morning, and Dewey had the fleet underway by 2:00 p.m.

By April 30, the fleet reached the entrance to Subic Bay, a sheltered body of water that Dewey expected to be the Spanish point of resistance. Controlling Subic Bay would be crucial to protect his badly stretched supply lines. He sent two ships to scout Subic and found nothing. The Spanish fleet was absent, the fortifications half-finished and abandoned. Little did he know that Spanish admiral Patricio Montojo had arrived at Subic Bay five days earlier to find the same situation—with equal surprise. The Spanish admiral expected to have a fortified position ready to prevent the Americans from getting anywhere close to Manila. Instead, he limped back to Manila to make his defense under the city's guns.

Entering Manila Bay would not be easy. The entrance is pocked by a collection of islands: the legendary bastion of Corregidor, Caballo Island just to its south, and a tiny spit called El Fraile (little more than a rock with a fort covering its entire surface). There are only two channels through which you can sail these islands: the two-mile-wide Boca Chica to the north and the three-mile-wide Boca Grande to the south. Dewey chose to travel by night through the larger but less charted Boca Grande to minimize the risk from shore-based guns. Just like his mentor Farragut, Commodore Dewey expected to be sailing through some level of mines—and was likewise willing to gamble that long immersion in tropical waters would have rendered those mines less than reliable.

The fleet entered Boca Grande by 11:30 p.m. on April 30. The passage began quietly under the darkness of cloudy skies and a new moon. But a few minutes after midnight of the fateful May 1, the small batteries on El Fraile opened fire, landing shells between USS *Raleigh* and USS *Petrel*. A brief exchange of fire ensued and El Fraile went silent after firing only three shots. Corregidor and Caballo remained conspicuously quiet. Dewey later theorized that the garrison commander expected the fleet to be unable to navigate Boca Grande without maps or experienced pilots familiar with the narrow waters.[11] The exchange claimed only one life: the chief engineer of the Coast Guard cutter *McCulloch*, who died of a heart attack from the stress of the exchange and the oppressive heat of nineteenth-century engine rooms.

Between midnight and 5:00 a.m., the fleet slowed to a crawl, barely making way, to allow dawn to illuminate the location of the Spanish fleet. The *McCulloch* and the supply ships were sent to a far corner of the bay to escape damage and allow maximum space for the warships to operate. As the sun rose on the morning of May 1, Dewey found no Spanish vessels near the Manila defenses. At 5:05 a.m., the batteries in Manila opened fire. The fleet unleashed a token reply, but Dewey was solely focused on the Spanish ships. Shore-based guns were dangerous but immobile; they could be dealt with later. The US fleet continued sailing south. It had been a long, tense night on the decks of the American fleet.

At 5:15 a.m., the fleets spotted one another. Admiral Montojo had arrayed his seven-vessel fleet in crescent formation in shallow water near Cavite City, the citadel southwest of Manila. He did this ostensibly to save crewmen's lives in case any ships sank. This was a noble goal, but it kept his fleet immobile and vulnerable. The American Asiatic Fleet sailed to within five thousand yards, despite shelling from the Cavite citadel, to improve the accuracy of its guns.

I can assure you that five thousand yards is very close for a big ship gun duel, especially when your opponent has the added advantage of supporting shore batteries. And when you are at the end of an impossibly long supply line, with no local resupply locations readily available for fuel or ammunition, the scope of options narrows swiftly. Every sailor and officer in Dewey's fleet would have known they had to strike and win or face a very uncertain situation. Dewey would have seen the guns of the Spanish ships quite clearly swiveling in his direction, and at that close range the muzzles of the enemy guns would have looked crystal clear through a pair of binoculars. This was the moment of decision, when it was for Dewey to set the example for calm, sensible command in the epic battle that was about to unfold. For the best of decision-makers, this is when you must force yourself to consciously feel time beginning to slow down. Like Farragut, George Dewey was over sixty years old. He sported an enormous handlebar mustache that made him look a bit like a walrus with a particularly piercing gaze. But his voice was steady and his eyes focused on the enemy ships.

At 5:40 a.m., Dewey uttered his famous phrase as an order to his flag captain as he looked at the stationary targets of the Spanish fleet: "You may fire when ready, Gridley."

For two hours, the Asiatic Fleet and the Spanish exchanged fire. USS *Olympia* led the fleet as it crossed the Spanish Line back and forth five times. The Spanish had more ships and the support of shore-based guns, but the US Asiatic Fleet boasted larger guns than their counterparts. Many Spanish ships were antiquated and slow: the second-largest ship in the fleet, *Castilla*, had to be towed to move, and Admiral Montojo's flagship, *La Reina Christina*, was made primarily out of wood and still had rigging for sails.

By an hour into the fight, it was clear that Dewey's superior gunnery, armor, and mobility were going to carry the day. At 6:30 a.m., with still no significant damage to the American fleet, the shells began to land on the Spanish ships with regularity and precision as the gunners found their range. The Spanish ships were brutally pummeled. Dewey continued to direct concentrated fire at individual Spanish warships, and eventually *La Reina Christina* and *Don Juan de Austria* attempted to break out of the immobile position to engage the Asiatic Fleet at point-blank range. But their bravery was overmatched by the ferocity of American gunfire, which forced the Spanish ships back into the shallows. Through the early hours of the battle, smoke obscured the damage to the enemy fleet.

At 7:35 a.m., Commodore Dewey received what would turn out to be a false report that his ships were running low on ammunition. His concerns about a protracted conflict with Spain came back into the fore given logistic challenges, so he chose to withdraw to a safe position to redistribute ammunition as needed. As far as he could see through the obscuring smoke of battle, the Spanish fleet was still intact and capable of further combat. To keep the men's morale high, he informed them that they were only withdrawing to have a leisurely breakfast.

But behind the smoke, the Spanish fleet was reeling. Most of the ships were on fire and sinking. *La Reina Christina* was almost entirely disabled, half of her crew were casualties, and her captain died from his wounds as he heroically directed rescue efforts. *Don Juan de Austria* was burning. The *Castilla* had only one operational gun out of six. Admiral Montojo was forced to relocate his flag to the *Isla de Cuba*, a ship one third the displacement of the *Reina Christina* and one fifth the displacement of *Olympia*. By 9:30 a.m., Montojo knew he would lose the battle.

At 11:16 a.m., Commodore Dewey discovered that the

supply message that forced the break-off had been garbled. Instead of having only fifteen *remaining* shells per gun, the fleet had *expended* only fifteen shells per gun. After serving the promised breakfast, Dewey turned the fleet back to its grim work against the Spanish fleet. The smoke had cleared, and he could see the damage the guns had inflicted. Now the firing resumed with devastating effect.

By 12:30 p.m., the Spanish surrendered. The figures were the most lopsided in the history of the US Navy. The US fleet suffered only seven injuries through the entire battle. Sadly, in addition to the chief engineer of USS *McCullough*, it suffered one death: Captain Charles Gridley of USS *Olympia*, who died of an illness just a month later. For the Spanish, the battle was a material and human catastrophe. Every ship sank, with 371 casualties out of nearly 1,500 combatants. With no ships left to threaten his US Asiatic Fleet, Dewey mopped up the rest of the static defenses. On May 2, the citadel at Cavite surrendered. Corregidor followed suit on May 3. Manila would not fall until August 13, after a 10,000-strong US Army force arrived in the Philippines to support the Filipino rebels fighting the Spaniards for independence.

News of the startling victory electrified the population of the United States and shocked the world. Manila Bay was the first US naval victory over a foreign power in 170 years. Dewey was a national hero both for his personal bravery and his remarkable results. For the rest of the world, it was a herald that the United States had graduated from a regional to a global power, able to project deadly force seven thousand miles from its Pacific shores and humiliate a European colonial power in the process. And it inaugurated a troubled colonial relationship with the Philippines whose echoes last to this day.

For Dewey, it would be the pinnacle of his career. The country was swept by "Dewey Delirium." His face was everywhere: in magazines, newspapers, and patriotic posters. Pictures with his Chow dog, Bob, whom he adopted while in Hong Kong, single-handedly made the breed popular in America. He was given his long-denied promotion to rear admiral, retroactive to the date of the Battle of Manila Bay. Congress and the White House created a special rank for him, the title of admiral of the Navy, in March 1899. Like his hero Farragut, Dewey held his unprecedented rank for life—but while the Navy had many admirals after Farragut, none have worn the six-star-equivalent rank since Dewey. He was so popular that he sought to run for president as a Democrat to unseat the president who had given him his command. But the Dewey Delirium was not to last, and several political missteps killed Dewey's presidential ambitions before they ever truly gathered momentum.

Instead, Dewey became a sage graybeard for the Navy. He devoted the rest of his professional life to the Navy's General Board, created in 1900 to be an advisory board to the secretary of the Navy. He would lead this board through the massive naval investment by President Theodore Roosevelt, his political patron, whose exploits in Cuba during the Spanish-American War helped win him the White House. Dewey's service on the board helped lay the intellectual planks for the US Navy's global orientation.

What made George Dewey decide to bring the fight to the Spanish when he was so far from any support and others were warning him that the Spanish fortifications were impregnable? There is an easy answer: he was following his orders to engage the fleet as quickly as possible. But the telegram he received from the secretary of the Navy was broad—the epitome of what the military calls "mission specific orders," meaning no set timeline or planning guidance. The urgency to strike was mostly Dewey's. So why the aggressive confrontation?

In large part, Dewey was reprising Farragut's "damn the torpedoes" gamble when he chose to go through the Boca Grande channel despite the rumor of mines and the lack of good charts. His aggressive attack against the Spanish fleet off Cavite demonstrated his belief in initiative as superior to fortification, which bore out in practice. He did not wait for

Washington to tell him that war had been declared with Spain; he preemptively moved the *Olympia* to Hong Kong to be prepared to bring the fight to the Philippines. He did not ask for permission to loiter in Mirs Bay; he just relocated there to wait for the consul with his much-needed information. And he purchased his two supply ships while in Hong Kong because it was what he needed to do the job.

But Dewey's initiative was not born out of ignorance or reckless aggression. Like Farragut, Dewey had studied and prepared aggressively before sailing into battle. His dogged fights with the Navy staff to get more ammunition before leaving for Asia gave him enough supplies to operate so far from support. He waited in Mirs Bay for the consul general to arrive so he could make educated decisions about how to approach Subic Bay and Manila. He used vessels to scout Subic Bay to ensure it had not been fortified. He searched Manila Bay methodically to find the Spanish fleet, even while under fire from the shore batteries. These measures of process and patience were the foundation that allowed his initiative to thrive. He later wrote in his book that "it was the ceaseless routine of hard work and preparation in peacetime that won Manila."

That ethos of preparation as the basis for bold action has become embedded in the US Navy as an operational force. From my earliest days at sea, I have heard captains say variations on the old military maxim that "tactics are for amateurs, logistics are for professionals." Every captain I served under could tell you off the top of his head the fuel in the ship, the number of missiles and gun rounds, and the status of the combat systems—including outstanding repair parts. The captains know where their next loads of fuel, ammo, and general stores are going to come from, and when they will arrive. An obsessive culture of training for the crew is very much part of Dewey's legacy of preparation. When I served in my first at-sea command, USS *Barry*, I required all the data mentioned above to be delivered to me freshly annotated every morning with my first cup of coffee.

At the same time, Navy commanders in the twenty-first-century fleet look for opportunities to move swiftly when the moment of decision arrives. As a strike group commander leading over ten thousand sailors and a dozen warships while embarked in an aircraft carrier, I was proud to watch the destroyer and cruiser captains under my command actively moving their ships into firing positions. Few waited for direction from the flag officer in the carrier; they wanted to be best positioned to be ultimately selected to launch the Tomahawk missiles or anti-air weapons to defend the high-value units in the strike group. The captains I most valued (and to whom I gave the best reports of officer fitness) were the ones who did both—focused on the preparation of their commands but operated with dynamic strokes even in the absence of specific direction.

In particular, I remember one of my destroyer captains—a woman who went on to make admiral—who had a reputation as a stickler for logistics. She would send very cogent assessments with great detail about the state of her anti-air AEGIS missile system, the readiness of her Tomahawk battery, the capabilities of her forward gun mount, the state of the ship's gas turbine engines—on and on. She often drove my staff crazy with her persistent demands for logistic support. But she was also very aggressive in how she maneuvered and placed her ship in combat situations, and always followed her instincts in taking on the tough situations at sea. After one boarding operation in the Arabian Gulf in 2003–04, she ended up capturing a group of very dangerous terrorists and after the takedown held them successfully aboard her ship for interrogation. Her name was Cindy Thebaud and the name of her destroyer, appropriately enough given her penchant for action and appetite for risk, was USS *Decatur*. As I watched her progress throughout the rest of a very successful career, ending as a two-star admiral and a strike group commander herself, I was struck by her ability to balance both high levels of preparation and boldness in action.

Dewey provides a powerful approach to decision-making

for us all. In a nutshell, his life and experiences tell us that our best decisions come when we combine a knack for somewhat mundane logistics and administration—the kind of person who would make a good head of the Navy's Lighthouse Board commission, for example—with the ability to strike boldly when the moment arrives. The better prepared you are, the bolder your decisions can become. There is a widely known Roman proverb that "fortune favors the bold." What many people do not know is that Tacitus, one of Rome's great writers, wryly remarked that "fortune favors the prepared," likely because he saw too many of his countrymen making hasty decisions that panned out poorly. Dewey's true strength was that he exhibited the sentiments of both aphorisms. He was very prepared to be bold, but at the right moment, which arrived through his preparation. It was a formula that made him both a national and a naval hero.

CHAPTER FIVE

The Protector

———•———

Cook Third Class Doris "Dorie" Miller,
United States Navy

Crew Member, USS West Virginia *(BB-48)*

ATTACK ON PEARL HARBOR

DECEMBER 7, 1941

"For distinguished devotion to duty, extraordinary
courage, and disregard for his own personal safety
during the attack on the Fleet in Pearl Harbor"[1]

In the summer of 1979, I was stationed in Newport, Rhode Island. At the hardly senior rank of lieutenant, junior grade, my job was to attend an eight-week course to become a steam engineer on an aircraft carrier, USS *Forrestal*. Before arriving in Newport, I had spent most of the previous three years in the high-tech end of the Navy as the anti-submarine warfare officer on a brand-new *Spruance*-class destroyer. But the Navy, in its wisdom, had decided I would head off to a very old aircraft carrier and be sent deep belowdecks to lead the engineers of a high-pressure steam plant in the hot, sweaty main propulsion spaces. Since I knew absolutely nothing about how a steam engineering plant worked (my new destroyer was powered by advanced gas turbines), the Navy had decided to send me to the Naval Training Command in Newport for a couple of months to study the mysteries of steam propulsion.

Newport in the summer was (and remains) quite fine—jazz festivals, minor league baseball, one of the last remaining grass-court tennis championships in the United States, all the beautiful mansions, and very nice beaches. The problem for me was learning how steam plants worked at sea. In a nutshell, fresh water is boiled in a huge tank, or boiler, and the resulting steam—full of energy—is blasted across massive engines that in turn drive the propellers that push the ship through the water. After exiting the engines, the steam turns back into water and is pumped through the cycle again. That sounds easy, right? Except that the steam is kept at high pressure (around 1,200 pounds per square inch) and passes through massive pipes. Under such pressure, steam will exploit even the smallest weakness in a pipe—and escaping steam can easily kill a person. Even when the steam stays in the pipes, all that superheated metal routinely keeps the surrounding air well over 100 degrees Fahrenheit. "Staying hydrated" doesn't begin to get at what a day in a Navy steam engineering plant is like.

You can learn the basics in the classroom, but to really understand what a steam plant is like, you must go to an actual operating plant. So, after a couple of weeks of classroom studies, my group of young officers was bussed over to the piers at Naval Station Newport and shepherded aboard a "training ship." This meant that the engineers on the training ship would show us around, teach us the basics, then let us try to run the plant. I wasn't looking forward to spending the better part of each summer day belowdecks in a steamy plant for the next several weeks, but in order to get ready for my next assignment it was something I had to do.

When we pulled up on the Navy bus in front of the training ship, I glanced at the brow skirt (a sign on the plank leading to the ship), which read USS *MILLER* (FF-1091). I wasn't impressed. The *Knox*-class frigates were notoriously difficult ships with a single screw propeller and an unreliable engineering plant, not very handy in a rough seaway, and seriously under-armed with a single main gun mount forward and a short-range anti-submarine rocket launcher. As we trooped aboard, I idly wondered who the Miller of the name might be. The only Miller I could think of was the famous playwright and author Arthur Miller (he wrote *Death of a Salesman* and was one of Marilyn Monroe's husbands, neither feat seemingly qualifying him to have a ship named after him). At the time, when I thought of Miller, it was generally to order a Miller High Life, the "champagne of beers."

As I stepped onto the quarterdeck and saluted the officer of the deck, I noticed a large black-and-white picture of a tall African American sailor in his dress whites. He was standing in front of a four-star admiral, Chester W. Nimitz, who was pinning a medal on him. The scene rang a vague bell. Pearl Harbor? After I got home that night, I dropped by the base library to work on an unrelated article about ship handling, but I couldn't get USS *Miller* off of my mind, so I pulled down a few reference books and articles and started to learn the story of Petty Officer Doris "Dorie" Miller. It is a powerful tale, full of inspirational grace notes, but also inextricable from the old, segregated Navy backstory: as a Black sailor in the early 1940s, the options were extremely limited in terms of what you could formally do on a ship. The high-tech specialties of communication, gunnery, navigation, and engineering were closed to African Americans; in fact, the only jobs they were permitted to do were cooking, cleaning, and serving as valets for the senior officers in the ships. It must have been demoralizing duty.

But then came war. As all hell broke loose in the Pearl Harbor, Hawaii, naval station basin under overwhelming Japanese aerial attack on a quiet Sunday morning on December 7, 1941, Petty Officer Doris Miller on USS *West Virginia* made a hard choice to risk it all. He left his relatively safe duty station in the wardroom belowdecks and made his way to the bridge, which had been strafed. There he found his mortally wounded commanding officer. As the citation for his Navy Cross says, "While at the side of his Captain on the bridge, Miller, despite enemy strafing and bombing and in the face of a serious fire, assisted in moving his Captain, who had been mortally wounded, to a place of greater safety, and later manned and operated a machine gun directed at enemy Japanese attacking aircraft until ordered to leave the bridge." He was wounded, constantly exposed to enemy fire, but he kept firing the gun, hoping he would shoot down a Japanese attack aircraft—which he may well have done. As I read the material, I wondered about him. What led him to charge to the sound of the guns? Was it instinctive? Or part of a long-held desire to show what he could do in the most demanding of situations? I learned that he was an athlete who played football in his Central Texas high school and went on to become the boxing champion on the battleship. Was that part of his decision, that competitive spirit?

Over the next several years, I continued to read and learn about Petty Officer Miller, and my esteem only grew. He was lost at sea and declared dead just a couple of years after Pearl Harbor, dying in an attack on his next ship, USS *Liscome Bay*, a small carrier, in November of 1943. But the roots of his story are part of the profound and painful African American experience in this country and are well worth understanding today. As my group of engineers in Newport went back over the next several weeks to the training ship USS *Miller*, I thought to myself that a frigate was far too small a symbol to encompass the story of Doris Miller. Flash forward forty years: the Navy's decision in 2020 to name the nation's next nuclear aircraft carrier for Petty Officer Miller is a very good one, and I am sure he would be stunned to know that his hard decision on December 7, 1941, would one day lead to his name being attached to a 100,000-ton nuclear-powered carrier.

Doris "Dorie" Miller was born on October 12, 1919—the third of four boys in a family of sharecroppers in McLennan County, Texas (near Waco, hardly a metropolis itself). McLennan County was a dangerous place for an African American family in that era. Just three years prior to Dorie's birth, thousands of residents—including the mayor—had turned out to watch a notorious lynching in Waco. But the Miller family endured on the fringes and tried to make a good life for themselves despite appalling treatment and deep institutional and cultural racism.

To call Dorie a "gentle giant" would seem a simplistic cliché, but in many aspects, the term fit him. At six feet three inches and 225 pounds, Dorie towered over others, especially in the mid-twentieth century, when the average American man would have been just over five feet eight inches tall. He was a good football player, but he had a mild demeanor and kind disposition that his Navy colleagues would remark upon throughout his entire career. Dorie did his best in school under the guidance of his mother. But being an African American male in McLennan County was, in Dorie's words, "going nowhere."[2] The family struggled to eat during the Depression, and Dorie dropped out of high school in 1938 to help support the family. The twenty-year-old enlisted in the Navy in 1939 in equal parts to find more viable employment and to escape the legacy of Jim Crow in McLennan County.

The US Navy was strictly segregated at the time of Dorie's enlistment, limiting all men of color (principally African Americans and Filipinos) to menial duties as messmen and the enlisted ranks. Ranking even below cooks, messmen prepared simple meals, set the table, did laundry, and shined shoes. Ironically, many Americans do not appreciate that the Navy was more integrated *before* the end of the Civil War than after it. Eight Black Union sailors received the Medal of Honor. The US Navy continued its practice of recruiting, retaining, and releasing Blacks for war and other national emergencies through much of the nineteenth century, but racial segregation and discrimination retrenched throughout the military as Reconstruction ended. As opportunities closed, the proportion of African Americans in the Navy fell by half—from 20 percent to 10 percent—by the

1890s.[3] The infamous *Plessy v. Ferguson* Supreme Court case came next, providing legal cover for discrimination under the banner of "separate but equal." The final blow was struck during the Woodrow Wilson administration, which segregated the entire federal government in 1913—codifying the Navy's resegregation in the process. Not even the exigencies of war would change the policy. During World War I, all people of color were limited in terms of the jobs they could hold and were barred from officer ranks. And while Secretary of the Navy Josephus Daniels did open opportunities to women during that time, only fourteen of the eleven thousand who served were Black. It was one of many sad chapters in our Navy's and nation's history for African Americans.

Dorie received his training at a segregated facility at Norfolk, Virginia, from September to November 1939. He then served in several initial assignments, first heading to the ammunition ship *Pyro* and then to the battleship USS *Nevada*. But his main home in his Navy career would be the battleship where he would make his hard choice: USS *West Virginia*. After he arrived, he tended to junior officers, serving their meals, doing their laundry, and waking them up in time for watches. But he found other outlets for his energy and desire to prove himself in his new environment. In his afloat career as a boxer, Miller was inferior to no one: he bested all comers to earn the heavyweight championship among the *West Virginia's* entire crew of several thousand.

In the background, tensions continued rising between the United States and Japan over the ongoing war in China and the seizure of French colonies in Southeast Asia. The United States reconstituted the Pacific Fleet in January 1941 and headquartered it at Pearl Harbor, where the peerless natural port of Oahu, near Honolulu, had served as a maritime hub since before the Hawaiian monarchy. By February 1941, the Navy ordered *West Virginia* to Pearl Harbor as part of a show of force to deter Japanese aggression against the United States. But American planners did not know that at that very moment Japanese naval planners were already hatching a scheme to attack Pearl Harbor. After long preparation, the Japanese were ready to strike in December of 1941.

At 6:00 a.m. on December 7, Dorie Miller woke up to do some menial work before enjoying a well-deserved day of leave. He chose to spend the day on the ship with a friend who had just gotten out of the brig, rather than taking up another offer to go ashore.[4] History might have been very different if he had chosen to get some time on liberty in Honolulu. But on a quiet December 6, planning to stay aboard the next day with a shipmate had been an easy choice. It was how he chose to respond to the surprise attack the next morning that would define the rest of Miller's life and his legacy.

The Japanese planes began their attack on Pearl Harbor at 7:48 a.m. By 7:57 a.m., the *West Virginia* was pummeled by a series of air-dropped torpedoes and armor-piercing bombs. The deck was soon burning from gasoline. During general quarters all crew members had a predetermined battle station. Miller's assignment involved handing ammunition to the anti-aircraft gunner. By the time Miller reported to his general quarters station in the wardroom, the damage to the ship was so severe that he decided he needed to pitch in to respond to the attack and left his battle station looking for action.

Put yourself in the mind of this young sailor from central Texas. It is his first moments in combat, and the ship is filled with the smell of cordite and racked by bombs landing both on board and on nearby sister battleships. It would have been utterly disorienting, and nothing in his background or training would have prepared him for this moment. Unlike Dewey or Farragut, he was not a mature man with multiple combat and sailing experiences under his belt, nor did he have any obligation to demonstrate to his subordinates his courage and determination—he was the most junior of sailors in the thousands assigned to the ship. Yet around 8:00 a.m., he decided to move from a place of safety, take a huge amount of personal risk, and do all that he could for the ship and his crewmates. From all accounts, both from those observing him and in his own words, he simply felt the need to protect and defend.

By perhaps 8:15 a.m., the bridge of the ship was shattered by incoming fire, and the commanding officer was gravely wounded. Miller, who had headed topside to do what he could, encountered a young officer, Lieutenant (later Admiral) Claude V. Ricketts. Ricketts was rushing to try to save the life of the *West Virginia*'s captain, Mervyn Bennion, and together he and Miller helped remove him to a lower-level bridge. The rescue team of Ricketts and Miller had to battle through a burning bridge and the ship's severe sideward tilt while chaos swarmed in the air and seas around them.

By 8:54 a.m., the second wave of Japanese fighters struck the fleet. Lieutenant Junior Grade Frederic White saw two nearby unmanned anti-aircraft guns, and he and Miller started loading the weapons for eventual use. After loading both guns, around 9:10 a.m., Miller—although untrained in the use of the gun—jumped into the gunner's seat and began cranking the barrel skyward toward the Japanese aircraft. Peering through the gunsight, he began to fire, swiveling the gun and leading the incoming aircraft despite continued incoming attack. Several accounts of his actions by officers indicated amazement at both his facility on the gun and the raw courage he demonstrated. By roughly 9:30 a.m., he had no ammunition left. After the battle, he cited his history of squirrel hunting as the source of his natural aptitude for gunnery.

With all the ammunition expended, Miller and White returned to Captain Bennion's side around 9:45 a.m. A team of four people tried with great difficulty to extract the injured captain from the tower below the bridge and bring him safely down to the main deck. With fires closing in around them, the group tried to use a ladder to lower him down but were unable to do so because the ship was listing too far to its port side. Captain Bennion heroically ordered them to leave him behind, but the team instead used a hose to fight the fires and stall for time. Sometime just after 10:15 a.m., two hours into the ordeal since the bridge was effectively destroyed, Bennion succumbed to his wounds as the rescuers continued to battle the flames.

At around 10:30 a.m., without a captain to protect, Miller and the others realized they needed to evacuate to the main part of the deck. But by this point, they were surrounded by fire and could not escape. They were saved by another sailor who threw a line from a nearby crane. Miller and his shipmates had to pull themselves fifty feet, hand over hand, above the fire raging in that part of the deck. Even after escaping the flames, Miller did not leave the stricken ship; instead, he worked alongside several other shipmates who were still unwounded to pull sailors out of the water covered in burning oil onto the relative safety of the deck as the ship continued to slide lower in the water.[5] Miller saved multiple lives in the process, a testament not only to his bravery but also to his superb physical condition and strength.

Dorie Miller must have been exhausted, dehydrated, and perhaps disoriented. There were multiple moments when he could have left the ship, and many of the crew did so, even though no formal "abandon ship" order had been given. The death of the captain and others in the chain of command caused many sailors to make their escape from what increasingly looked like an inferno. Yet Dorie Miller stayed until the *West Virginia*'s acting captain gave the order to abandon ship around 2:00 p.m. Miller was one of the last people to make his escape. The last group of survivors swam the length of three football fields to get to nearby Ford Island. Only from shore did Miller finally have a chance to look back and survey the burning ship, take in the widespread destruction in the harbor, and let the day's events catch up with him. In all his later interviews and talks with family, he attributed his survival to divine providence and God's intervention. By 3:00 p.m., he knew he would survive the day—one that would indeed live in infamy.

Why did Miller make the choices he made? Under surprise attack, a flight response would have been understandable for most of the general population, and he would have been justified in simply staying out of the line of fire, as most of the crew did. The tranquil Sunday morning became a blazing inferno in minutes. The water itself was on fire, burning from slicks of oil loosed from the dying ships. The noise was deafening, and enemy fire rained down from every direction. And the circumstances only got worse the deeper Miller went into the infamous morning hours. His world was off-kilter, quite literally given the dramatic list of the ship. Instead of choosing safety, Dorie Miller chose to keep pushing forward from crisis to crisis throughout the entire ordeal. He was fortified by his training as a sailor, to be sure, but clearly there was something deeper that propelled him throughout that day and compelled him to remarkable action.

His decision is all the more remarkable because of the context. Beyond the human instinct to flee for safety, he, like many of his fellow sailors, had been specifically and systematically treated as a second-class citizen of his native country and his Navy. Messmen served an essential role aboard ships, but not a valued one; they were not only outranked by everyone else aboard but frequently also despised or resented despite their toil. Why, then, did Miller stay aboard and fight for his ship—and his all-white officers—on a day when many sailors tried desperately to swim to safety?

It surely had to do with more than a desire to support his family: if a steady paycheck remained the goal, swimming to shore immediately would have been the best bet. Nor could Miller have expected fame and glory: though he became an early icon of the World War II civil rights movement, he could not have known that when he leapt into action in 1941. As no less a judge of human behavior than Napoleon observed more than a century before Pearl Harbor, "A man does not have himself killed for a half-pence a day or for a petty distinction."

Was Miller just following orders? To an extent, certainly: he went first to his normal duty station, and then to the bridge alongside an officer to help rescue the captain. Back on deck after their daring escape from the bridge, there were certainly senior officers trying to organize a response amid all the chaos. But from jumping on the gun himself to staying on the burning deck to the bitter end, Miller consistently took initiative—and personal risk—far beyond the scope of any orders he received. Again and again, he risked his life.

Patriotism, commitment to his ship and its crew, and defeating the enemy played a central role. After the battle, survivors spoke of their hot-blooded desire to fight back against their Japanese attackers. But the famous gunnery episode comprised mere minutes of Miller's hours-long ordeal aboard the *West Virginia*. If he was only trying to shoot back at the surprise attackers, then he would have gone overboard as soon as his weapon ran out of ammunition. Something beyond circumstance, orders, or the heat of battle must have driven Miller's decisions as he tried to extricate his commander, swung back down to the main deck, and continued to aid his fellow crewmen in their desperate attempts to escape.

In my estimation, Miller's defining decisive trait was his desire to protect others. He did so over and over again in his life: by blocking and tackling on the football fields of Central Texas, by volunteering into the segregated Navy when he and his family needed any kind of an opportunity, and, on that infamous day, by going far above and beyond the call of duty. He was in every sense a "protector," and his choice on that day was grounded in his desire to do what he could for others. It is a classic example of the Greek warrior code from the ancient Spartans—that the opposite of fear on the battlefield is not courage; rather it is love—love for your fellow man and woman. Dorie Miller showed that on December 7, 1941, in every way.

When the Navy released the stories of heroism during the battle, Miller's actions were recounted in detail, but his name was not initially published. He was referred to only as an unidentified messman. But fellow sailors who had seen him in action soon spread Miller's story through informal networks, and his heroism galvanized public sentiment back home when reported by the *Pittsburgh Courier* and other outlets in the Black press. Groups like the National Association for the Advancement of Colored People (NAACP) and National Urban League trumpeted Miller's selfless service in spite of unequal treatment and helped elevate Miller in the public consciousness alongside Joe Louis, the heavyweight boxer who challenged racial stereotypes and who was involved in many wartime public relations campaigns. The Roosevelt administration seized on Miller's example to promote African American enlistment in the coming war effort. As his name and fame continued to spread, Congress began to consider awarding him the Medal of Honor. Though white legislators proposed the award for him in both the House and the Senate, the effort was ultimately stymied by Southern senators. Shamefully, Secretary of the Navy William Frank Knox also put his thumb on the scale to prevent the award.[6]

But six months later, Miller received the Navy's (as opposed to the nation's) highest commendation for performance in combat: the Navy Cross. He received his award personally from the commander of the Pacific Fleet, Admiral

Chester Nimitz, who was also the chief of all naval forces in the Pacific, during a ceremony on the deck of the carrier USS *Enterprise* in Pearl Harbor. The Navy also gave him an opportunity to enter a different, previously off-limits, specialty and further develop his marksmanship. Instead, Miller chose to be a cook—breaking the ordinary rank ceiling imposed by segregation but continuing to serve alongside the messmen. In interviews, he said he looked forward to opening a supper club after he got out of the Navy.

Sadly, the Hollywood ending was not to be. During the remainder of his service, the Navy failed to learn from Miller's example. He faced racism at least as fierce as before—along with new suspicion from fellow messmen. Like far too many exemplars before and since, Miller's rising stature outside the Navy was met with rising resentment within. After the Navy awarded Miller its highest award for gallantry, the officers and sailors around him all seemed to act as if they believed he had risen above his station. The institutional racism that had been built into the organization for decades was simply unable to embrace the clear example of real heroism right before their eyes. He sailed on and continued his life of service as the war unfolded, assigned to another ship after a string of war bond drives, recruitment campaigns, and civilian awards for heroism back on the US mainland.

Miller never had a chance to open his supper club. He

was transferred to the newly launched escort carrier USS *Liscome Bay* in June of 1943. Escort carriers were distinguished primarily by compromises in their construction: about as large as regular carriers, they were built with far less armor to speed production. They were officially designated CVEs—"carrier, escort" in the Navy's system of abbreviation—and sailors derisively but justifiably said that their designation stood for "combustible, vulnerable, and expendable." At 5:13 a.m. on November 24, 1943, near the Gilbert Islands in the South Pacific, the *Liscome Bay* was struck by a torpedo fired by a lone Japanese submarine. The resulting explosion was so massive that it lit up the morning sky and sent metal raining down on ships fifteen thousand feet away. Only two hundred people out of a crew of over a thousand survived the explosion—tragically, Cook Third Class Doris Miller not among them. His body was never found, and he was officially declared presumed dead one year later.

Miller's legacy lives on in the Navy to this day. Although there was obviously not an immediate racial epiphany after Pearl Harbor, initial steps toward integration in the Navy began after the death of Secretary Knox in 1944. James Forrestal, his successor, argued that a segregated Navy costs too much and he did not believe the stereotypes and racial beliefs justifying naval policy. As Doris Kearns Goodwin wrote: "The example of Miller's heroism became a principal weapon in the battle to end discrimination in the Navy."[7] Without his gallantry, it is hard to know when the Navy might have desegregated. He was someone that chief of naval operations Admiral Elmo Zumwalt mentioned personally to me in the late 1990s as an iconic African American sailor. I often show a picture of a Navy destroyer's crew taken in the late 1940s in which the messmen were made to stand at the back of the formation—we've come a long way since then. Admiral Michelle Howard, whom you will meet later in this book, was the third Black, and first woman, four-star admiral. April D. Beldo became the first Black woman fleet master chief in 2013. But there remains much to do. Overall, there remain few African Americans in senior ranks of both uniformed and civilian leadership in the Navy. Admiral Mike Gilday, the chief of naval operations, commissioned Task Force One in June 2020 to examine racism, sexism, and biases within the Navy. This is, I hope, the first step in the right direction for the Navy; it does justice to Miller's legacy.

When the ship that introduced me to the Navy's most heroic cook, USS *Miller*, was decommissioned in 1991, I was sad to learn the news, remembering Miller's heroism and wishing he was still underway with us in the fleet in the form of a warship named after him. Throughout my long career, stretching well over three decades since I walked aboard the *Miller*, I tried hard to remember his legacy and all that had been denied him and other African Americans. We need to ask ourselves relentlessly the question, "What are we doing today that in thirty years or so will look oh so wrong?" It is a question I tried to ask myself often in the Navy as I did all that I could to create change at each level in my career. It is a good question for anyone to ask themselves as they wrestle with hard choices, not just under fire in combat but in the quiet of a company's boardroom or mailroom, or in a police station in a small town, or in the congregation of a church, or on the faculty of a university. Dorie Miller made a hard choice on our behalf; we can offer no less than the same in return in the choices we make about our society.

Fortunately, we know now that Dorie's name will grace the seas once more on a magnificent *Ford*-class aircraft carrier sometime later in this decade. But there is one honor that still eludes him: the Medal of Honor. Giving Dorie Miller the Medal of Honor will not heal all our country's racial wounds. Much of the argument against his receiving the Medal of Honor centers around the ongoing disagreements about whether he shot down any Japanese planes or if his actions were sufficiently "above the call of duty" to warrant the medal. But much of the ongoing argument misses the point about what made Dorie Miller so noteworthy.

When faced with a circumstance where he could have kept himself safe while still serving in his role, Miller instead made a tougher, nobler choice. He rose above the barriers that society placed in front of him and put himself in harm's way for our country. We should give the highest honors to the people who make decisions like Dorie Miller. That is a legacy still unfulfilled, and a worthy goal for our Navy to seek.

Finally, we should ask what we can learn from Dorie Miller's hard choice at Pearl Harbor. I'd say it is that there will come a moment for all of us when the opportunity arises to take on a hard, unfamiliar task in order to help or protect someone else. For the vast majority of us, of course, it won't be in the middle of a combat situation. It may be at the scene of a car accident, or in a bar intervening to help an intoxicated person, or on a wintery sidewalk picking up someone who has fallen hard on the ice, or simply stopping what we are doing in a work cubicle or lunchroom to address a moment of real distress, to comfort another person. It is always far too easy to sort of edge off the stage when things are going wrong for someone we don't know well or toward whom we don't feel an intense connection. In those moments of decision, I think the lesson of Dorie Miller is simple: to stand and deliver, without any thought of personal gain. Heroism is taking risk on behalf of someone else when it would be easier to just pass on. Dorie Miller chose to put himself in danger and serves as an example of the hardest but best choices we end up making. His hard choice to stand and deliver in the riskiest of circumstances should call out to the best in each of us.

CHAPTER SIX

The World Wonders

———•———

Admiral William "Bull" Halsey,
United States Navy

Commander, US Third Fleet

BATTLE OF LEYTE GULF

OCTOBER 23–26, 1944

Hit hard! Hit fast! Hit often!

In the 1970s, I probably spent my happiest hours as a midshipman at the US Naval Academy in Halsey Field House, the cavernous multisport athletic facility just inside the gate. For me, frankly, Annapolis was not always a joyful experience. I found the discipline extremely repressive, the loss of personal liberty onerous, and the academics rigorous but seldom inspiring. But throughout much of the year, I could forget all my complaints about the Academy when I stepped on the varsity squash courts in the field house.

Squash is a funny game, at the time played almost exclusively in the Northeast of the United States, and I had never tried it before arriving at Annapolis. I had been a competitive tennis player throughout my youth, including winning a divisional championship my senior year in high school in Arizona. When I got to the Academy, I tried out for the tennis team and barely made it—nailing down the last spot at the bottom of the roster. Most of the players in my class and senior to me were taller and could cover the court better, and many of them simply had more racket skills. After a lackluster fall outdoor tennis season, the varsity tennis coach, Bobby Bayliss, pulled me aside and said, "Jim, you are never gonna be a top tennis player here. With luck you might eventually earn a letter. But you'd be a terrific squash player, I think. Try out this winter for the squash team. I think you'd be a better fit over there."*

So I dutifully arrived at Halsey Field House after the short fall tennis season and tried the game of squash. It is played indoors on a four-walled court, much like its more popular cousin racquetball. The rubber ball in the American style of the game at that time was small, very hard, and stung like hell when it hit you (which occurred far too often). The court is small enough that a player like me with speed and reflexes could, in most cases, overcome taller opponents with longer wingspans. It is a game of angles and corners, highly strategic, very aerobic, a kind of instantaneous vector analysis. And it is an underdog's game because you can outmaneuver and outthink more physically talented opponents. A friend once aptly described it to me as "brain

---

* I did eventually win a tennis letter—barely.

on brain" warfare. I spent hours every day on those squash courts, losing myself in the violent exercise and mental challenges of a sport I continue to play to this day—at a far slower pace, to be sure.

At the time, I didn't give much thought to Fleet Admiral Halsey, for whom the field house was named. But over time—as I took courses at Annapolis in sea power and military history—I began to appreciate the personality and decision-making style of Halsey, which in some ways reminded me of squash. He was an impulsive, instinctive warrior who did not agonize over any given decision. Indeed, a lot of his victories early in World War II (such as Guadalcanal) were the result not so much of luck, nor of a deeply conceived battle plan, but rather fast and certain decisions, violently executed. In fierce combat with the Imperial Japanese Navy, Halsey placed his forces squarely in the flow of events—which is how most squash players win in the crucible of a sport where the ball moves at close to 200 miles per hour, your opponent is in the close fight with you, and there simply isn't time to ponder every nuanced point.*

Another aspect to appreciate about Halsey was his willingness to embrace the newer and riskier elements of the Navy. Throughout the bulk of his career, he was a classic

---

* Only in the sport of jai alai does a ball move faster in a game where players are on a court and at risk of being hit.

surface warfare officer, focused first on torpedoes and destroyers, then on the big-gun warships of his era, the heavy battleships and cruisers. But when the chance came to join in developing the new domain of naval aviation, Halsey seized it. He was fifty-two years old when he earned his wings of gold as a full-fledged naval aviator and remains today the oldest person ever to qualify.[1] It wasn't a carefully thought-out career strategy, by the way, but rather a spur-of-the-moment decision to make the jump when offered it by his mentor, Fleet Admiral Ernest King. His wife described him as an "old fool" for taking on the longer and more dangerous aviator course when he had originally been going to do the much shorter and safer naval observer course.

I learned many lessons in instinctive decision-making on the squash courts of Halsey's namesake field house, where I won a lot of matches for Navy and eventually was ranked near the very top of the ladder. As a team, we finished in the top five in the country two out of the three years I played on the varsity squad, and I lettered each year, beating Army twice. In those close-fought matches, I also learned—as Halsey knew—that when the velocity of the game demands decisions at instinctive speed, not all those decisions will break in your favor. In the climactic Battle of Leyte Gulf, Halsey's decision to take the powerful Third Fleet north to meet a Japanese decoy fleet was arguably the worst of his career and almost ended in disaster. However, he made those decisions consistent with the skills and persona of the leader and officer he was, and never looked back.[2]

In his brilliant book about the Battle of Leyte Gulf, *Sea of Thunder*, historian and journalist Evan Thomas catches well the kind of decision-making Halsey favored:

> Who can know what it is really like to stand, bone-weary, on the bridge of a ship in action, responsible for hundreds if not thousands of lives, unsure of the enemy's strength and whereabouts, yet forced to make fatal decisions? In any culture, there are warriors who meet timeless and universal standards of courage and resolve, who do not seem to need to think or ponder or question—who know, instinctively, when to lay their lives and those of their men on the line. That is not to say their judgment is always correct, just that their bravery cannot be denied.[3]

Fleet Admiral Halsey was such a warrior.

There is a powerful lesson in that, but a dangerously seductive cautionary tale as well. In many situations, it just feels right to "trust your gut." But the real skill of decision-making lies in finding the balance between carefully analyzing options with infinite care while scoping risk, versus simply deciding to cut the Gordian knot and move out. As twentieth-century columnist and satirist H. L. Mencken supposedly said, "For every complex problem there is an answer: clear, simple, and wrong."

In Halsey's case, there were many times when high-speed, instinctive decision-making worked in his favor, notably in the beginning of the war. But at other times, as at Leyte Gulf, that clear and simple approach went terribly wrong. He felt goaded by forces beyond his control at times, including an unfortunately ill-timed and badly worded naval message from Fleet Admiral Nimitz, his boss, at the critical moment in the battle.[4] Decisions made in stress and at speed are fraught with danger; for the naturally exuberant and impatient Halsey, temper and impulse could easily get the better of him.

Halsey was not a squash player, by the way, but rather a fullback on the Annapolis football team, and a pretty good one.[5] Lord Wellington supposedly said, "The battle of Waterloo was won on the playing fields of Eton." It might be an apocryphal line, but there is some truth in the idea that competitive sports—where decisions must be made at speed and accepting of consequences for good or ill—do help prepare us for the more consequential choices we face later in life. While I can make the case that taking all the time available to make key decisions is generally the right approach, my time on the squash courts in Halsey Field House, alongside the example of Fleet Admiral Halsey, helped me along the voyage of my life when there simply wasn't lots of time to ponder the options. I am no "Bull" Halsey in so many ways, but there are many times when I've tried to summon up his ability to choose *now*, and vow not to look back in anger or regret, no matter the outcome.

It's said that blood is thicker than water, and that has long been true of the Navy. Deep as the love of the sea might run in any officer's veins, seafaring—and especially naval command—has often become the business of families for generations. Stephen Decatur's father was a naval officer, and David Farragut's natural and adoptive fathers were both naval officers. William F. Halsey Sr., whose namesake would go on to stardom as a fullback at Annapolis and then as one of the five-star fleet admirals of World War II, was also a naval officer. Incidentally, my own family follows the pattern: my father was a Marine officer, my wife's father was a naval officer, and one of our daughters and her husband have also served as naval officers.

William F. Halsey Jr. was born on October 30, 1882, in Elizabeth, New Jersey. Bill, as he was called throughout his life, aspired early to the naval life. ("Bull," by the way, was an appellation of the wartime press, but it suited Halsey's persona so well that it is widely remembered three quarters of a century later.) Young Halsey met no strenuous objection from his parents, but he did struggle to obtain an appointment to the Naval Academy, which was effectively the only entry point to the tight-knit society of naval officers in those days.

After initial setbacks but no less determined, Halsey enrolled at the University of Virginia, intending to study medicine and back-door his way into the Navy as a physician. After finally receiving an appointment to the Academy in 1900, thanks to a direct supplication by his mother to President William McKinley, Halsey leapt at the chance to put on a midshipman's uniform and subject himself to the harsh conditions of a service academy. He regretted leaving behind at UVA the woman who later became his wife, Frances "Fan" Cooke Grandy, but she promised to wait for him through the four-year commitment at Annapolis, and she did.

His solid football career was not the most important part of Halsey's time at Annapolis. The crucial element of attending the Naval Academy in those days was becoming integrated in the naval fraternity of the still-small interwar fleet. Annapolis sowed the seeds of a fertile and lifelong network: "almost all top naval commanders of World War II . . .

had been midshipmen together at the academy between 1901 and 1905."[6] These officers included Halsey's boss, Fleet Admiral Chester Nimitz; his alternate in command at sea, Admiral Raymond Spruance; and his counterpart at the climactic Battle of Leyte Gulf, Admiral Thomas Kinkaid. It is worth noting, by the way, that today the cerebral Spruance enjoys a better professional reputation overall than Halsey, even though his quiet persona left him behind in the competition for media affection. He ended up as "only" a four-star admiral, though he never breathed a word of resentment about his more heralded contemporary.[7]

After graduating from the Academy, Halsey began his career at sea as most ambitious officers of his time did, in battleships. Though he would command at the absolute height of a navy larger than any other the world has seen before or since, Halsey commissioned into a small US Navy that was just beginning to stretch its sea legs on the global stage. As a young ensign, he sailed with the famous Great White Fleet that President Theodore Roosevelt sent on a round-the-world cruise in 1907–09. Returning to the United States, he was promoted straight to full lieutenant, skipping over the junior grade of that rank. At around the same time, the strains of sea duty were beginning to show in his marriage to Fan. The couple was not destined for long-term happiness: tragically, Fan suffered from manic depression from the 1930s onward, at times so severely that she could not live at home with Halsey and their two children.

In time, Halsey moved from battleships into destroyers and then even smaller torpedo boats, and he earned a Navy Cross for his service in command of the destroyer USS *Shaw* during World War I. The interwar years saw Halsey ascend through a range of roles ashore and afloat, including as naval attaché in Berlin (like the famous literary captain Pug Henry in Herman Wouk's masterpiece *The Winds of War*), in command of destroyers at sea, and as commander of the (immobile) station ship at the Naval Academy. After that tour in Annapolis, Halsey went back to sea in destroyers once more, and then back ashore to attend the Naval War College in Newport.

His big break finally came in 1934. Admiral Ernest King, then the head of the Navy's growing Bureau of Aeronautics and destined to become the most powerful naval officer in US history as chief of naval operations and commander in chief of the US fleet during World War II, offered Halsey command of the aircraft carrier *Saratoga*—on the condition that Halsey earn his wings. Halsey agreed with gusto. Although the shorter and safer naval flight observer qualification would have sufficed, he opted instead for full qualification as a naval aviator. After successfully landing an airplane on a carrier deck, Halsey earned his wings on May 15, 1935. Fan, having come to the reasonable conclusion that this was folly, wrote to their daughter: "What do you think that the old fool is doing now? He's learning to fly!"[8]

At age fifty-two, Halsey remains the oldest person ever to earn the golden wings of a US naval aviator. But he was no fool, at least as to the future conduct of naval warfare. He is reported to have said that "the naval officer in the next war had better know his aviation, and good." Regardless of whether he ever in fact uttered those exact words, the insight was correct. Then as now, the Navy required that officers in command of aircraft carriers be qualified aviators, and Halsey and King were not the only members of their Annapolis classes to run that gauntlet relatively late in life. The next war would indeed require admirals who could not only command at sea but also understand and apply air power.

And, of course, it was the naval air forces of the Japanese Empire that plunged the United States into World War II with the surprise attack on December 7, 1941. Although the attack on Pearl Harbor wreaked havoc on the battleship fleet that was tied up pier side on a Sunday morning and on the planes parked wingtip-to-wingtip at the airfield, the

Navy was not mortally wounded. Fortunately, Halsey and the aircraft carriers were safely out to sea, returning from a mission to reinforce the tiny Marine garrison on Wake Island (where naval intelligence had indicated a surprise attack might be imminent). Halsey got lucky on the return journey, when foul weather kept the carriers out to sea a day longer than planned, thereby just missing the Pearl Harbor attack. Weather affects all sailors, of course, but encounters with the rough storms of the Pacific would become one theme of Halsey's service throughout the war, both for good and for ill.

As the country mobilized for war in the days and weeks after Pearl Harbor, the Navy had big questions to answer. How had it "allowed" the surprise attack to happen? And how could it bring the fight to Japan, even as the bulk of the nascent war effort was directed toward Europe?

Halsey was out in front as the Navy sought to answer both questions. First, he testified in support of his old friend and Annapolis classmate Admiral Husband Kimmel, who had been in command of the Pacific Fleet at the time of the Pearl Harbor attack. After the attacks, Kimmel was relieved of command and called before a commission to determine culpability for the surprise. Halsey testified before the commission that he also had not believed the Japanese would attack Pearl Harbor. He then joined Admiral Chester Nimitz, Kimmel's replacement as commander of the Pacific Fleet, and other senior admirals in Pearl Harbor to discuss how best to strike a blow against the Japanese. While some of those officers did not feel the Navy was ready to counter-attack yet, Nimitz wanted to attack as soon as possible to demonstrate that the Navy was still vital and capable. Ever aggressive, Halsey not only loudly backed his new boss's plan but volunteered to lead the attack himself.[9] Halsey's gumption earned him Nimitz's lasting gratitude and placed him in the thick of the action as the United States went to war in the Pacific.

The first action came in the Marshall Islands in the early days of February 1942. At enormous risk, Halsey sailed the *Enterprise* battle group past several Japanese-held islands and then remained on station off the Marshalls for a couple of days, launching dive-bomber attacks against the Japanese and dodging enemy bombs in return. The raid accomplished remarkably little of military value, but it was a vital morale boost. Screened by another lucky storm system at sea, Halsey sailed safely back to Pearl Harbor and a hero's wel-come. War correspondents, in need of a tough protagonist and captivated by Halsey's half-smiling, half-snarling after-action press conference, "lost no time at all enshrining him as the nemesis of the Japanese, a half-fictitious character whom they named 'Bull Halsey.'"[10]

Like Halsey's persona, the press hugely inflated the effects of the Marshall Islands raids. Pearl Harbor was hardly avenged, and the US Navy was still just getting organized as a true combat force and remained a shadow of the warfighting juggernaut it would become. As March 1942 wore on, various plans were discussed between Washington and Pearl Harbor, all with the goal of landing more punches against the Japanese. Ultimately, these coalesced around the boldest plan of all: the bombing raid on Tokyo launched by Army pilots in Army planes from the decks of carriers commanded by Halsey. Halsey set sail from Pearl Harbor with utmost secrecy on April 8, 1942; ten days later, James Doolittle's heavily laden bombers barely lumbered aloft from the carrier decks and flew into history. Although their bombs did little damage, the audacity of the raid was a huge boost to American morale and pushed the Japanese into vengeful paroxysms. When Halsey and the carriers returned to Pearl on April 25, they were not cheered for launching the raid, as the details of the "impossible" mission were kept secret throughout the war in order to keep the Japanese guessing. Even President Franklin Roosevelt got in on the game, suggesting at a press conference that the bombers had launched from the mythical island of Shangri-La.[11]

Halsey himself was in no mood to celebrate. Gaunt and showing the strain of command at sea, he also suffered terribly from a severe case of dermatitis. With his skin itching and painfully peeling all over his body, Halsey was eventually forced by doctors to go back to the mainland for rest and treatment in San Francisco. Halsey's illness prevented him from leading the fleet into the dramatic Battle of Midway in 1942. Spruance sailed instead and inflicted a crushing defeat on the Japanese. Midway is also the battle most celebrated by today's US Navy and is regarded, like Trafalgar, Lepanto, and Salamis, as one of the great pivot-point battles in history. Although Halsey was furious at missing the fight, he recovered his health, and he and Spruance would continue to serve in lethally effective alternation throughout the war.

Fortunately for Halsey, there was still plenty of combat ahead, with thousands of miles, hundreds of islands and atolls, and more than three years until total victory. Cured at last of his skin condition, Halsey flew back out from San Francisco to take up a new post as commander, South Pacific, replacing his old friend and Annapolis football teammate Admiral Robert Ghormley. Halsey established his headquarters at Nouméa, New Caledonia, in October 1942, in the midst of desperate and uncertain fighting on Guadalcanal Island. He immediately made clear that the Marines on the island would stay there and defeat their Japanese opponents. Two days later, he instilled his fighting spirit throughout his entire command when he passed an order abolishing the uniform necktie for all sailors and Marines serving in the South Pacific. It might seem a small thing, but it delivered a big morale boost and epitomized Halsey. The "Bull" caricature might have been somewhat embellished, but the correspondents who peddled it had plenty of material to work with.

Throughout 1943, the South Pacific was the ring in which the US and Japanese navies punched and counterpunched. As the Solomon Islands campaign raged, naval airpower continued to show its dominance, and Halsey continued to show his doggedness. "As long as I have one plane and one pilot," he barked to a staff officer, "I will stay on the offensive."[12] In November, with a chance to smash a Japanese cruiser force, Halsey launched the most daring carrier raid since Pearl Harbor. The results were staggering—not only were the Japanese heavy cruisers sunk in the harbor of Rabaul, but Halsey's aviators did more damage ashore than many had thought possible against such a well-defended target. The raid risked more than carriers and aircraft; had it failed, the upcoming amphibious landings on Bougainville beginning in November 1943 would have been woefully unprotected. Halsey later recalled this as the narrowest scrape of his time in command in the South Pacific.

As the calendar rolled over to 1944, fighting shifted

to the Central Pacific—and into a still-higher tempo. By then, the initiative had passed decisively to the Americans, and they intended to make the most of it. US industry came fully alive, sending ships, planes, and materiel to the front in incredible quantities. A streamlined and effective training pipeline allowed men (and some women) to apply that material might against the Japanese. Halsey and Spruance rotated in command so as never to give the enemy a break. The fleet remained at sea, simply changing designations from Third Fleet to Fifth Fleet and back again as the two admirals swapped in and out.

Spruance remained in command of the fast carrier task force throughout much of 1944, giving Halsey and his closest aides, known as the "Dirty Tricks Department,"[13] more time to rest and plan ashore. Meanwhile, US objectives and lines of command were shifting throughout the Pacific. As the fleet grew in size and the Japanese began to fall back before the onslaught, the Joint Chiefs decided to prioritize a direct advance across the Central Pacific. In June, the American and Japanese carrier forces fought each other directly for the last time in the Battle of the Philippine Sea. Although the Americans came out ahead, several of the enemy carriers got away, and the Imperial Japanese Navy lived to fight another day. Soon after, Spruance rotated ashore and Halsey retook command at sea. The Fifth Fleet became the Third Fleet once again and was directed to support the massive American landings on the Philippine island of Leyte. What remained of the Imperial Japanese Navy was marshaled to oppose the Americans, and the stage was set for the largest naval battle in history—and the most remembered and fateful decision of Halsey's career.

The US invasion of the Philippines began on October 20, 1944. General MacArthur waded ashore just after 1:00 that afternoon, strode up the beach, and announced by radio to the people of the Philippines that he had returned. Over the ensuing days, US forces continued to pour ashore under the watchful eyes of their naval screening force, including Halsey and the Third Fleet. Confusingly, the Leyte operation involved two numbered US fleets, the Third and the Seventh, each of which reported to different chains of command. Halsey's Third Fleet answered to the Navy command in Pearl Harbor and Washington, while the Seventh Fleet, under Admiral Thomas Kinkaid, was tasked to Army General Douglas MacArthur. Almost three full years of war with Japan had still not resolved the tensions and contradictions between the various branches of the US armed forces: although they had the same ultimate goal, the Army-directed landings were barely coordinated with the Navy's efforts to defend the landings from Japanese attack in the surrounding seas. The confusion was to have nearly disastrous consequences in the coming days and was a part of the decision-making matrix that dogged Halsey.

Against the overwhelmingly large but dangerously disorganized US forces, Admiral Soemu Toyoda decided to commit the last strength of the Imperial Japanese Navy. With precious few naval aircraft or competent pilots left after the "Great Marianas Turkey Shoot," as US pilots called the destruction of Japanese naval air forces during the Battle of the Philippine Sea, the only big punch he had left to throw was the enormous naval gunnery power of the Combined Fleet's remaining battleships and cruisers. For good measure, he also decided to send the carriers in a separate thrust, though they would serve more as tempting bait for an aggressive commander than as a major offensive force in their own right. All told, Admiral Toyoda deployed a formidable force from the Combined Fleet's remaining redoubt in Brunei, but he, too, failed to establish a coherent command structure among the Northern Force (the carriers) and the Center and Southern Forces (the striking surface combatants).

The Battle of Leyte Gulf began just after 1:00 a.m. on October 23, when the US submarines *Darter* and *Dace* spotted and reported the Center Force, including the two largest battleships ever built, the *Yamato* and *Musashi*, as they steamed slowly into the entrance to the Palawan Passage southwest of the major Philippine Islands. After radioing this contact to the Seventh Fleet, the two submarines charged ahead, submerged, and unleashed a large spread of torpedoes against the Japanese ships. Two heavy cruisers, including the flagship, blew up and sank in a matter of minutes; another had to retire from the action with heavy damage. The Japanese commander, Vice Admiral Kurita, was plucked from the water and reestablished his command in the super battleship *Yamato*.

Halsey spent the twenty-third preparing to fight. His ships refueled and rearmed at sea, then steamed westward to seek out and destroy the Japanese. As morning broke on the twenty-fourth, planes from both sides found each other. American search planes radioed Kurita's position back to their carriers, but the carriers of Task Group 3 soon found themselves under attack from land-based Japanese aircraft. Though the task group's fighters dispatched most of the attackers, one bomber slipped through, scoring a direct hit on the carrier *Princeton*, which burned for six hours before exploding with great loss of life just before 3:30 p.m. Meanwhile, Center Force was pounded by aircraft from Task Group 4, a separate group of US carriers that did not come under attack from Japanese planes. The American fliers of Task Group 4 delivered a shellacking: *Musashi* took nineteen torpedoes and over a dozen bombs, three other battleships and a light cruiser were moderately damaged, and a heavy cruiser was forced to leave the fight. At about 3:00 p.m., Kurita—unable to make contact with his counterparts to the north and south, and his ears no doubt ringing from the day's fighting—decided to back off rather than proceed through the San Bernardino Strait and into the teeth of more American aircraft. By 7:35 p.m., the mighty *Musashi* finally succumbed to her wounds, rolled over, and sank.

Just as Kurita was pulling back, however, Halsey was charging ahead. Ironically, the one group of Japanese ships the Americans had failed to spot all day was the carriers of the Northern Force, in spite of the latter's desperate efforts to be found. The Japanese commander sent his fastest ships racing south toward Halsey, whose planes finally spotted them at 4:00 p.m. Flying back along the faster ships' track, the American pilots finally spotted the four Japanese carriers at 5:00 p.m., and "the one piece missing in the puzzle" at last fell into place.[14]

This is the moment in which Halsey's belligerence, determination, and above all bitter hatred for the Japanese carrier force came into play. Like a fullback hitting a hole in front of him, he effectively blocked out everything else and drove forward. He didn't stop to think about his assigned mission of protecting the landing force. As soon as he received the report of the Japanese carriers' whereabouts, the always-aggressive Halsey set course due north to destroy them. This was the moment of decision that reflected Halsey's impulsive spirit, and which would haunt him for the rest of his life. The decision might have been in the spirit of his orders, which encouraged him to destroy the main body of the enemy fleet, but it was a huge gamble. With Halsey's Third Fleet heading north to hit the carriers, and Kinkaid's Seventh Fleet positioned far to the south blocking the Southern Force's advance through the Surigao Strait, the US landing force off Luzon was left wide open to attack by the Center Force should Kurita reverse course and sail through the San Bernardino Strait.

Compounding Halsey's error in deciding to take his entire force north to attack the enemy carriers was his inept communication with his fellow commanders. He was unclear about his decision to take the entire force because earlier in the afternoon, around 3:15 p.m., as he was still searching for the Japanese carriers, Halsey had sent a telegraph to his subordinates stating that a powerful surface force—designated Task Force 34—would detach from his attacking fleet. The message was not clearly worded, but it was received and read by Admiral Kinkaid (to the south, in command of Seventh Fleet), Admiral Chester Nimitz (Halsey's boss, in Pearl

Harbor), and Admiral Ernest King (the Navy's top admiral, in Washington, DC)—all of whom assumed that Halsey had formed Task Force 34 and left it at the eastern outlet of the San Bernardino Strait to cover his carrier-chasing action. He had not.[15] The landing force was protected only by a handful of destroyers, destroyer escorts, and a few light carriers.

In fact, as Halsey clarified in a subsequent message at 5:10 p.m., Task Force 34 would only detach on his express order. Since he had not yet passed the word, the ships of Task Force 34 were steaming north with the rest of Halsey's force. And because he sent this clarification by voice radio rather than telegraph, no senior US commander in the Philippines, Pearl Harbor, or Washington read this addendum or connected the dots. When Kinkaid received a message from Halsey at 8:00 p.m. saying that Halsey was "proceeding north with three task groups to attack carrier forces at dawn," he assumed Halsey was referring to his three carrier groups and had left a detached fourth group—Task Force 34—behind. The landing force was essentially naked, and the Japanese heavy surface force was closing.

As October 24 rolled over into October 25, miscommunications and misunderstandings began to compound. Kurita did in fact turn back and risk the San Bernardino Strait, only to find it unguarded. He sailed through and was spotted by a US surveillance plane. Halsey received a report on Kurita's action, but did not turn any part of his force back to block the advancing Center Force. Halsey's subordinates grew increasingly nervous, but also did not challenge their commander directly. Staff officers woke Vice Admiral Marc Mitscher, Halsey's air commander, to implore him to convince Halsey to turn around, but Mitscher responded, "If he wants my advice, he'll ask for it" and went straight back to sleep.[16] Almost simultaneously, around midnight, Kinkaid's battleships utterly destroyed the Japanese Southern Force in the Surigao Strait, but Kurita's Center Force emerged undetected and unmolested into the Philippine Sea. As Kinkaid turned to congratulate his officers on a smashing success, Kurita turned south and bore down on the unprotected US landing force.

Halsey finally gave the order to form Task Force 34 at 2:40 a.m. on October 25, only to send it out ahead of his carriers to shell the Japanese while US planes attacked overhead. At 4:12 a.m., Kinkaid radioed Halsey to inquire specifically as to the whereabouts of Task Force 34. It took almost three hours for Halsey to read and respond to this message. At 7:00 a.m., just as Halsey was beginning his attack on the Japanese carriers hundreds of miles to the north, Kinkaid read with a chill that Task Force 34 was still steaming north with Halsey. Kinkaid barely had time to worry. At

7:20 a.m., the radio waves filled with calls for help from the only ships left to oppose Kurita's southward thrust—the tiny escort-carrier forces known by their radio call signs as Taffy One, Taffy Two, and Taffy Three. The men of these destroyers, escort carriers, and their air wings confronted the powerful Japanese force with utter heroism and desperately broadcast pleas for help from any larger forces in the area. Although Halsey could hear their distress calls, he still pressed his attack against the Japanese carriers. For Halsey, the world had narrowed to the single task ahead of him, destroying enemy carriers. The echoes of Pearl Harbor and the chance for vengeance against the hated carrier force effectively blocked all other considerations from his mind. He had decided and would not waver.

As the destroyers of the Taffy force continued their desperate and near suicidal fight against the massive Japanese battleships and cruisers, Halsey's superiors grew deeply concerned. By 8:00 a.m., both Admiral Nimitz in Pearl Harbor and Admiral King in Washington, DC, were pacing their offices. By 9:45 a.m., Nimitz could stand it no more: the Taffys had kept up the fight longer than anyone had any right to expect, and Task Force 34 was nowhere to be found. Breaking with his usual practice of noninterference with a commander in battle, he dictated an inquiry to Halsey: "Where is Task Force 34?"

What was only a five-word query in Pearl Harbor became one of the most infamous messages of the war. Nimitz's radiomen first emphasized the admiral's message with a repeat, then encoded it, including random "padding" phrases at the beginning and end, as was standard. As received by Halsey's radiomen, the message read "TURKEY TROTS TO WATER . . . WHERE IS RPT WHERE IS TASK FORCE THIRTY FOUR RR THE WORLD WONDERS." Halsey's communicators correctly removed the initial padding phrase "turkey trots to water," which preceded the message's addressing information. But they left the unintentionally apt final phrase—which followed the doubled consonant "RR" signifying the end of the message—and handed their commander a slip of paper with the question: "Where is, Repeat, Where is, Task Force 34, The World Wonders!"[17]

At 10:00 a.m., with his team, Halsey read the message and exploded. The bridge of his flagship flowed with volcanic rage at the enormous and apparently personal critique behind the question. Not until his chief of staff, later admiral Mick Carney and a future chief of naval operations, directly confronted him did Halsey begin to regain control of himself.[18] Meanwhile, his force continued steaming northward—carriers, battleships, and all. If Halsey realized he had made a critical mistake, he went right on making it for over an hour. Finally, just as his surface ships were within range of the Japanese carriers, Halsey ordered them to turn south at 11:15 a.m. By then, the destroyers of Task Force 34 needed to be refueled at sea, so the entire force delayed for another couple of hours before steaming south together. It was 1:00 p.m. and too late to salvage the situation to the south. But here luck played a role, alongside the heroic attacks of the small destroyers.

By the time Task Force 34 was finally riding to the rescue, the battle was all over. Convinced by the ferocity of the Taffy destroyer attacks that he had run into one of Halsey's main carrier groups, and with no word from the Northern Force, Kurita stopped his attack to regroup and, at 12:30 p.m., telegraphed his high command that he was retreating back the way he had come. Four hours later, with all four Japanese carriers sunk, Halsey threw another belated punch: he detached the fastest surface ships in his force and sent them southward in relief. Although they overtook the slower ships of Task Force 34, this relief force was in time only to pick up survivors from the Taffy squadrons and to sink one straggling destroyer of the mighty Center Force. The invasion was secure, but Kurita had slipped away with nearly all of his ships. Halsey had made a bad decision, compounded it with his personal pique and anger, and, fortunately, was reprieved by an equally bad decision on the part of the suddenly timid Japanese admiral.

The ships of the Taffy destroyer force became instant legends in the surface Navy and were immortalized in a brilliant book written decades later by famed naval historian James Hornfischer. Entitled *The Last Stand of the Tin Can Sailors*, it features the particular heroism of Native American commanding officer Ernest Evans of the destroyer force. We met him in the introduction to this volume, and alongside several other ships and hundreds of sailors who perished in the fight, his name lives on in the annals of naval combat leaders.

By nightfall on the twenty-fifth, the major actions of the Battle of Leyte Gulf had concluded. There were several codas—including the first use of kamikaze aircraft against the hapless Taffy escort carriers as Kurita retreated—and a few more Japanese ships were sunk by US submarines. But the strategic results were clear: the US invasion of the Philippines was secure, and the fate of the Japanese Empire was sealed. Though the war would continue on land and sea through almost ten more months of increasingly desperate violence, the loss of the Philippines also meant the end of material imports from Japan's remaining colonies in Southeast Asia. The Imperial Japanese Navy would never seriously challenge the US Navy again, and, from November 1944 until the atomic bombs fell in early August 1945, the Japanese war effort was slowly strangled to death while its citizens suffered terribly under strategic bombing campaigns.

Fortuitous as this outcome was for the war effort, it was lost on no one that the men and ships of the landing force, to say nothing of the additional months and lives a prolonged campaign might have consumed, had been saved *in spite* of Halsey's decisions, not because of them. Questions, accusations, and recriminations began almost as soon as the shooting stopped and have continued through hundreds of histories written since. How had it come to pass that such a popular and successful commander had performed so badly at one of the most important moments of the war in the Pacific?

The questions only grew louder some weeks later, when Halsey chose not only to stay out at sea but also to keep the Third Fleet sailing close together in spite of (admittedly conflicting) reports of an impending typhoon. Halsey inadvertently steered his armada into the very center of the storm on December 17, and by the time the Third Fleet reemerged a day later, it had suffered three destroyers sunk, nine other ships damaged, more than a hundred aircraft destroyed on deck or washed away, and nearly eight hundred men drowned. Known to meteorologists as Typhoon Cobra and to the US Navy as Halsey's Typhoon, this was the worst of Halsey's many run-ins with storms at sea. Almost as soon as it was over, Halsey faced a court of inquiry in the presence of his boss, Admiral Nimitz; though he was found responsible for an "error of judgment," Halsey was not officially censured for his actions. Nimitz, known for leniency toward his subordinates, kept the popular and inspiring Halsey in the fight—but command of the fleet at sea passed back to Admiral Spruance in January 1945.

Halsey rested until May, then resumed command of the fleet from Spruance. In June, he sailed the fleet into another typhoon, which caused further loss of aircraft and men. Once again, Halsey faced a court of inquiry; this one explicitly recommended he be removed from command, but Nimitz overruled the court and kept Halsey at sea. Halsey commanded the Third Fleet through the end of the war and once again launched airstrikes on the Japanese mainland. Had the atomic bombs not ended the war, Halsey would have supported the Allied invasion of the Japanese home islands; as it happened, the instrument of surrender was signed on the deck of his flagship, USS *Missouri*, on September 2, 1945.

Returning to the United States, Halsey was selected as the fourth of four admirals to receive a fifth star for World

War II service. Promoted to the rank of fleet admiral on December 11, 1945, Halsey remained in uniform until March 1947, though as a fleet admiral he technically remained on active duty for the rest of his life. Halsey died while vacationing in New York in August 1959. After lying in state at the National Cathedral, he was buried next to his parents in Arlington National Cemetery. Fan survived her husband by nine years and was buried beside him in 1968.

What are we to make of the complicated and compelling, impetuous yet effective character of "Bull" Halsey today? In particular, what lessons can we draw from his decision-making during the critical hours of the Battle of Leyte Gulf, when nearly a full day's worth of poor communications and decisions badly risked hundreds of ships and thousands of lives?

For better or worse, Halsey's service in World War II shows that a successful style of bold decision-making can earn enormous trust and responsibility. Early on, Halsey was a fighter when the Navy, especially the newly appointed Admiral Nimitz, desperately needed one to shake off the shock of Pearl Harbor. The "Bull" Halsey persona created after the symbolic Marshall Islands attacks of February 1942 by the extremely sympathetic press of the day was the perfect answer to the public's clamor to know where the Navy was and what it was doing. Similarly, Halsey's popularity with the sailors of the Third/Fifth Fleet gave Nimitz a strong argument to keep Halsey in command even after he lost so many ships, planes, and men in the typhoons of December 1944 and June 1945. In this way, Halsey was perhaps the Navy's nearest analogue to the Army's General Douglas MacArthur, a towering personality to whom the ordinary rules consciously did not apply. Halsey was never as overbearing as MacArthur, nor did he cross the red line into domestic US politics, but he was a political and strategic asset to Admiral Nimitz and the Navy's top commanders in Washington throughout the war. No one better exemplified the warrior spirit of the US Navy during the greatest trial by combat in its history.

Halsey's service provides some important reminders about both the benefits of hindsight and the perils of unchecked ambition and aggression. Halsey sailed into the Battle of Leyte Gulf with orders to destroy the main body of the Japanese force if he could, and with the memory of Admiral Spruance's "failure" to do just that at the Battle of the Philippine Sea fresh in mind. Though most historians agree that Spruance made the right call, Halsey "didn't want any damn super-cautious business tied to him."[19] At Leyte,

Halsey assumed the carriers still constituted the main force of the Japanese navy, and under no circumstances would he lay himself open to criticism for hanging back.

Even if he could not have known just how bare those carriers' decks were, though, Halsey's eagerness to destroy them (and thus outdo Spruance) led him to ignore the information that reached him through the night of October 24 and into October 25, as well as his subordinates' growing and explicit misgivings. War happens quickly and mistakes are inevitable, but Halsey repeatedly failed to adjust his tactics or mindset to the changing picture of events, steadfastly maintaining after the war that he had made the right call. He did not, and his tunnel vision in pursuit of Pyrrhic victory at the cost of near catastrophe should serve as a stark reminder against refusing to admit new information, fighting the last battle, or getting too carried away with one-upmanship.

Halsey's struggles with communication at Leyte remain sadly relevant to us in the Information Age. Halsey was in some ways not set up for success with the lack of unified command and communication between his Third Fleet and Kinkaid's Seventh, even as they were supporting the same operation. But Halsey made several grave errors of his own, from his confusing and ineffective messages about the creation, whereabouts, and mission of Task Force 34 to his slow responses (in both word and deed) to direct requests for help. Even if it was understandable, his tantrum in response to Nimitz's query was frankly inexcusable. We are all entitled to our feelings, especially in the heat of the moment, but taking questions or criticism too personally always runs the risk of clouding one's judgment at a dangerous moment. As Halsey's reaction demonstrates, flying off the handle never helps, and continuing to make a mistake out of spite or indignation can badly compound the initial error.

Still, the US Navy continues to venerate Halsey to this day not only because of the halo of victory in World War II, but also because his brash and confident personality is perceived as part of a winning organization. Halsey was a resilient fighter, whether against his own medical challenges or the incredible pressures of command in war. In this way, he follows in the tradition of Stephen Decatur and David Farragut, and presages the instinctive decisiveness of admirals who followed him in Korea, Vietnam, and the Arabian Gulf. Our images of leadership have become much more diverse, to be sure, but an indomitable character and a bias for action continue to mark the most outstanding leaders across eras and challenges. Just as John Paul Jones wished "to have no connection with any ship that [did] not sail fast" and the great British admiral Nelson said that "no captain can do very wrong if he places his ship alongside that of the enemy,"

Halsey's famous dictum to "hit hard, hit fast, hit often" encapsulates the decisive spirit that all great leaders must learn to channel. His decisions at Leyte Gulf were recklessly overaggressive, but the spirit in which he made them echoes on in our Navy today and helps many of us take bold action in challenging moments. Halsey's persona is not the right model for every situation, but his determination, resilience, and confidence are often key ingredients for victory. His spirit sails proudly on.

CHAPTER SEVEN

No Way Out

Lieutenant Commander Lloyd M. Bucher,
United States Navy

Commanding Officer, USS Pueblo *(AGER-2)*

SEIZURE OF USS *PUEBLO* BY
NORTH KOREA
JANUARY 23, 1968

Good intelligence is the life blood for successful
defense of our country.[1]

When I was a young commander in the Pentagon, I would often play squash with a retired vice admiral named Hal Bowen. He was a small, sprightly figure with a very good game considering he was then in his early eighties. He had contacted me through the squash coach at Annapolis, looking for challenging matches in the old Pentagon Officers' Athletic Club, a run-down sports facility with beat-up squash courts in the basement of the Pentagon. Admiral Bowen went on to win a couple of national championships in the over-eighty-five age group, which I found quite impressive—although he would say to me, "Heck, all you have to do to win a national title in your eighties on a squash court is stay vertical." He did a lot more than just stay vertical, and won his share of points in our matches, even though I was more than four decades his junior and had played on the varsity team at Annapolis.

After we finished and were chatting while cooling down, I'd ask him about his career. Like me, he was a destroyer commander with service in cruisers as well, and he had seen lots of combat in World War II and the Korean War. He gave me some good advice as I was thinking through what to request for my next sea command, which would be either a squadron of destroyers or an AEGIS cruiser. After giving me a thorough look at the pros and cons of destroyer squadron versus cruiser (he had served in three of each), we moved on to more general conversation. One day, I asked him a question I often asked very senior naval officers: "What really stands out to you in the course of your career, Admiral?" He looked up sharply and said simply, "I was the president of the court of inquiry for the *Pueblo* incident." That got my attention. A US Navy court of inquiry, for non-naval aficionados, is the courtroom proceeding to investigate possible acts that significantly violate navy regulations, such as a collision, grounding, sinking, or capture of a naval vessel. It is a very, very serious and rare event.

I encouraged him to talk about that experience, because I knew only the barest outlines of the story—that a small US Navy intelligence-gathering ship, USS *Pueblo*, had been seized by a North Korean naval force in the late 1960s. I had been a freshman in high school when it happened, and it registered on me at the time only because of my desire to go to Annapolis. Beyond the basic facts, including that the crew was held for nearly a year and brutally tortured before being released, I did not know much. I was vaguely aware of the name of the unlucky commanding officer, the then lieutenant commander Lloyd "Pete" Bucher. And I knew there was a great deal of controversy over the decision not to court-martial Bucher over his failure to fire even a single shot against the North Koreans. Instead, he surrendered the ship after being surrounded—even though he was indisputably in international waters. The whole incident was a long way from the standard Navy line of "don't give up the ship, and fight her until she sinks," the dying words of naval hero captain James Lawrence in 1813 on board USS *Chesapeake* in a battle with the British warship *Shannon*.[2]

For Vice Admiral Bowen, the case was brutally simple. Instead of following longstanding Navy tradition and fighting to defend the *Pueblo*, Bucher decided to turn the ship over to the enemy. Bucher said later he based his decision entirely on a desire to save the lives of his men. Admiral Bowen had clearly turned the case over in his mind many times and said to me, "Bucher could have been a great naval hero, but he lost his ship and all the intelligence on it. It was indefensible." He got an angry look on his face and said, "It was a mistake for the Navy not to court-martial that man. I understand that he wanted to save his crew and be humane and all that, but that's not the job we gave him. He was the captain of that ship, and he failed—plain and simple." I remember those words from twenty-five years ago as clearly as if he had spoken them to me yesterday. It was his tone, so cut-and-dried and matter-of-fact, that stuck with me. Vice Admiral Bowen was a warm and friendly man, and I had many good conversations with him over the years before his death in 2000. But that morning, in the heart of the Pentagon, his voice was cold as ice. "We don't give up the ship, Jim. That's tradition. And it's a tradition because so many people have *traditionally* made the *right* decision in combat. Some have paid the price with their lives. He did not."

Since then, I've often thought about the agonizing choice presented to Pete Bucher—to engage in a hopeless firefight against overwhelming odds, or to surrender and hopefully live to fight another day, knowing that the captivity would probably be terrible as well. There was no good way out of the situation. It is the kind of wrenching decision I never had to make, and I'm glad I did not. Like many naval officers, I like to think I would have responded with small arms fire and tried to get the *Pueblo*'s frozen machine guns functioning. But if I am honest with myself, I'm not so sure. Of all the choices in this book, I think Pete Bucher drew the worst hand of cards, and for the rest of his life he had to constantly defend his decision. The traditions of the Navy never ceased to weigh on him, and after he retired (as a full commander, about where he probably would have ended his career even absent the *Pueblo* incident), he continued to feel unjustly accused and unfairly judged by many. The story is a hard but sobering look at how we weigh our lives and the lives of our subordinates in the most dangerous of situations, and the echoes of the *Pueblo* reverberate today in the ethos of the Navy. Bucher's decision is worth examining in real depth, and we should honestly plumb the lessons with clear eyes and an open mind.

Lloyd M. Bucher was born in Pocatello, Idaho, in 1927. He had a rough start to life: his mother died not long after he was born and his adoptive parents, from whom he took his family name, Bucher, died when he was three. He spent parts of his childhood with his grandparents and with his vagrant father until becoming a ward of the state. He bounced around orphanages in Idaho, punctuated by a short-lived escape attempt, before gaining entry into the Boys Town home in Nebraska, which still serves today as a home for troubled children. He obtained the nickname "Pete" on the football fields of Boys Town[3] and would use it through the rest of his life. He was a wild child with a penchant for mischief, but he managed to graduate in the top ten of his class. Boys Town remained a lodestone in his life long after he left. He wrote glowingly in his autobiography about his connections to the institution, his pride at being the first alumnus to command a Navy ship, and the joy he felt when his priest-mentor from Boys Town traveled to Puget Sound for the commissioning of the *Pueblo*.

Bucher developed a boyhood passion for the ocean while with his grandparents in California. So when he graduated from Boys Town with good enough grades to go to college but no money, he saw his opportunity to prepare for his future by heading to sea. He enlisted in the Navy in 1946, having just missed World War II, and fulfilled his two-year obligation. He used his new funds to go to college at the University of Nebraska and was commissioned as an officer in 1953. At the start of his career, Bucher was a diesel boat submariner and loved every moment of it. He waxed poetic about the "elite group whose tightknit organization and un-matched esprit de corps had been for years a great source of pride for me."[4] To this day, the US Navy submarine force (now all nuclear powered) retains its own distinct culture, one of close team bonds, a fanatical dedication to perfec-tion, and just the slightest bit of endearing quirkiness.

Much to his dismay, Bucher did not remain a submariner throughout his career. After eleven years below the waves,

Bucher was "surfaced" to his first command role at age forty on USS *Pueblo*. He was extremely disappointed that he would not get to command a submarine, but he was happy to have a ship of his own, regardless of how prosaic the *Pueblo* seemed from the outside. Bucher found out later that his plodding vessel was part of Operation Clickbeetle, a clandestine program devised by the Navy and the National Security Agency. Clickbeetle would retrofit old cargo vessels into spy ships masquerading as science vessels. Bucher would be overseeing not only the sprucing-up of an old hull but the installation of some of the most sophisticated listening equipment the United States had at its disposal. This would in turn free up the submarines that were occasionally press-ganged into such missions to counter the rising power of the Soviet Navy under Admiral Sergey Gorshkov. The operation happened under the utmost secrecy. The listening equipment was sequestered in a special room with access granted only to a few Naval Security Group (NSG) officers and cryptology technicians. Most of the rest of the crew were initially largely unaware of the vessel's true purpose, although over time they probably formed a pretty good idea of what was going on.

The plan was for these ships to loiter in international waters off enemy coasts and obtain information on Communist countries during the height of the Cold War. These vessels would all be stationed in Japan for rapid deployment to three of the largest threats behind the Iron Curtain: the Soviet Union, China, and North Korea. The first Clickbeetle vessel, USS *Banner*, had been operating in the Sea of Japan since October of 1965.[5] The *Banner* encountered its fair share of close calls, including being surrounded by Chinese trawlers near Shanghai and having Soviet guns trained on it outside of Vladivostok. But the signals intelligence (SIGINT) that it collected was valuable enough that the NSG and NSA continued.

In the shipyard for conversion, Bucher learned what he could about his new mission while dealing with an endless stream of problems with the retrofit. The integration process was a mess, including an embarrassing incident where the electronic monitoring equipment was installed upside down. Bucher clashed frequently with his superiors about the state of the program and the lack of resources, whether it was effective destruction systems for classified materials or adequate watertight systems. His fights with leadership became so vicious that it ended up as a blemish on Bucher's annual performance evaluation. But these combative episodes were not just demonstrative of Bucher's pugnacious nature; they spoke to how deeply he felt responsible for his crew. That same evaluation noted, "He appears motivated solely by a keen sense of loyalty to his unit with the best interests of the navy uppermost in his mind."[6]

The people under his command were both intimidated and in awe of the "intellectual barbarian" who led them.[7] Bucher swore like a sailor (and drank like a sailor) but read extensively. He loved a good game of chess as much as he loved a competitive tussle in a bar. He would read the riot act to anyone who did a mediocre job on the ship, but he put his professional future on the line to get some of his enlisted sailors out of a run-in with military police. He instituted a policy to play the song "The Lonely Bull" every time the *Pueblo* entered or left a port. All in all, Bucher was a force of nature on the *Pueblo*, and his crew was happy that the storm was on their side.

After its troubled retrofit was complete, the *Pueblo* made its way to its home base in Japan by way of Hawaii, blaring "The Lonely Bull" into and out of ports along the voyage and leaving rowdy sailors' stories in its wake. From Japan, the *Pueblo* set out for the Korean Peninsula on January 11, 1968. From the beginning, the journey proved perilous. Powerful storms raged throughout the voyage around Japan, through the Tsushima Strait, and northward into the Sea of Japan. Even seasoned sailors were brought to their knees with seasickness. No doubt most of the crew thought this would be the most difficult part of their journey. Four days of rough sailing brought them to their first target along North Korea's border with the Soviet Union: the international waters off the port city of Chongjin.

On January 21, the *Pueblo* had made its way outside of another city, Mayang-do. The voyage so far had been uneventful, and the intelligence had been of limited value. Apart from the weather, the *Pueblo*'s first mission was appearing rather dull.

Unbeknownst to Bucher, events on the Korean Peninsula were slowly spinning out of control. Tensions had been rising along the Demilitarized Zone (DMZ) and adjacent waters since the previous year. Then, North Korean commandos covertly breached the DMZ on January 16, the same time that the *Pueblo* was moving on from Chongjin. The group's objective was to infiltrate the Blue House and assassinate South Korean president Park Chung-hee. The commandos were disguised as South Korean soldiers when entering Seoul, but local police challenged the group as it marched toward the Blue House on January 21. The ensuing firefight claimed the lives of South Korean police, innocent bystanders, and most of the would-be assassins. The few who escaped were ruthlessly pursued in a nationwide manhunt. Many in South Korea were calling for retaliation. Both sides of the DMZ were on high alert, waiting for the proverbial shoe to drop.

On January 22, the *Pueblo* had its first run-in with the locals. Two North Korean fishing boats investigated the *Pueblo*, withdrew, and then came back for a second look. Like their Soviet and Chinese cousins, fishing trawlers like these moonlighted as scouts and intelligence collectors for Pyongyang. But the two vessels were unarmed, which was a relief to Bucher.

January 23 was the fateful day. *Pueblo* loitered in international waters off the coast of Wonsan, the large North Korean port city that housed some of its submarine force. Bucher later wrote that he'd already started the day on the wrong foot. He woke at 7:00 a.m. with minimal sleep and running purely on his early-morning coffee. He coasted through an uneventful morning until lunch when they spotted a submarine chaser eight miles away on a direct intercept course. Bucher gave strict orders to keep most of the crew belowdecks and out of sight of the Korean ships to obscure the *Pueblo*'s true capabilities. Within minutes, the patrol craft was upon the *Pueblo*. Hoisting the signal flags that vessels use to communicate with one another, the North Korean warship threatened the *Pueblo*: "Heave to or I will fire."

Bucher was confused: "heaving to" means stopping forward movement, and the *Pueblo* was already bobbing peacefully per its oceanographic cover story. Bucher raised flags in defiance, identifying his position in international waters and intent to stay in the area. So far, this was shaping up to be a standard confrontational experience like those faced by *Banner*.

But things escalated quickly. Within half an hour, three fast torpedo boats were spotted coming from Wonsan, and by 1:00 p.m. they surrounded *Pueblo* on all sides with weapons trained on it. Minutes later, two MiGs were spotted overhead. The Americans were now surrounded in three dimensions.

Bucher considered his options and asked his crew if they could scuttle the ship, sending it to the bottom of the ocean with all her secrets aboard. But it would take more than two hours to do so, immobilizing the vessel and cutting off all communications with US forces in Japan for backup. Bucher's heart sank further when his crew reported the local depth: 180 feet. It was so shallow that North Korean divers could reach the wreckage and the information within a sunken hull. He would be stranding the crew in hostile waters in 20-degree weather for the sake of causing North Korean divers a minor inconvenience. In short, they were paralyzed, blind, surrounded by a superior force, and unable to communicate with their only source of help. Bucher's best shot was to get out of danger with his ship above the waterline.

After a ten-minute standoff, one of the torpedo boats pulled up alongside the larger sub chaser. Bucher spotted men armed with automatic weapons jumping onto the small vessel, which promptly turned directly toward the *Pueblo*. A boarding party.

Bucher decided he had enough. He signaled via flags his intent to leave the area and ordered the vessel to break out to sea at full speed. The *Pueblo* lumbered deeper into international waters, but the sub chaser and torpedo boats pursued with minimal effort. The sub chaser signaled again: "Heave to or I will fire." The *Pueblo* tried to adjust course to the south to put more distance between it and the sub chaser, but the chaser adjusted course to match. The cumulative rightward turns were starting to push the *Pueblo* on a direct course toward the North Korean mainland. The *Pueblo* continued to make a run for it while trying to present a minimized profile to its pursuers.

The North Koreans began to open fire, first from the sub chaser's 57 mm heavy machine guns, then from light machine guns on the torpedo boats. The first burst of armor-piercing rounds lasted about five seconds. Bucher knew for sure: the North Koreans did not care about international law or antagonizing a nuclear superpower. All they wanted was *Pueblo*.

Bucher gave the order to destroy all the classified material on board. The main burners were too small to handle the influx of paper, and the main incinerator was topside and exposed to enemy fire. The crowded hallways belowdecks were turned into spontaneous burn operations. Acrid smoke mixed with body heat as the crew coughed and clawed their way through destroying whatever they could. But the ruggedness of some of the machinery turned out to be a liability. Multiple sailors sustained injuries when their sledgehammers bounced off their targets.

Bucher did not order his crew to battle stations. His only armaments were some .50-caliber guns on deck, and those were carefully wrapped under tarps to maintain the vessel's veneer of scientific innocence. Preparing these weapons would have taken time, during which his crew would have been exposed to fire from both the sub chaser and the torpedo boats' machine guns. Even if the weapons were operational, they did not have any armor plating to protect the gunners. Bucher judged that the crew would be more useful belowdecks burning documents as fast as they could.

The pursuing ships continued firing bursts intermittently, riddling the *Pueblo*'s superstructure with holes and keeping the crew flat on the deck or well below. It is here that Bucher made his fateful decision: after receiving heavy fire for about seven minutes, he ordered the *Pueblo* to stop without firing a shot.*

The North Korean guns went silent, and they signaled for the *Pueblo* to follow them back to the mainland. Bucher paused for ten seconds, pondering what to do. He made a simple choice: stall for time. He put the *Pueblo* on the course to North Korea but only at one-third speed. This slower trip would allow the maximum time for US air support to arrive and for the crew to destroy classified materials aboard. Bucher ducked belowdecks to supervise the destruction. When he returned to the bridge, he was surprised to find that the *Pueblo* had increased its speed as requested by their captors. Enraged, Bucher gave the order to stop and stall for more time. The North Koreans immediately began shelling the vessel again until it picked up speed back to one third. This time, there were casualties. Numerous men were wounded, including Bucher himself, and the destruction operations belowdecks were slowed by injuries and gore. One fireman apprentice would be dead before the ordeal was over.

By this point, the North Koreans had had enough of Bucher's stalling. Two minutes after the second round of

---

* Bucher claims in his autobiography that his chief engineer made the decision to stop the *Pueblo*, but the engineer and the official court of inquiry claim that Bucher gave the order to stop.

bloody shelling, they sent their earlier boarding party to take the ship. Bucher put on his best clothes to meet the boarders and keep a semblance of naval tradition in the situation. But the boarders had other plans: the leader of the expedition put a pistol to Bucher's head the second that Bucher raised his voice in protest. They swept through the ship, asking through interpreters about the mission and their equipment belowdecks. Bucher or anyone else who repeated the oceanographic cover story was pistol-whipped.

Having taken the crew captive, the North Koreans put a civilian pilot aboard the *Pueblo* to bring the vessel to shore. What came after was a waking nightmare: Bucher and his crew were prisoners in North Korea. They were beaten, starved, and tortured for an agonizing eleven months. Their story is one of perseverance and heroism. While it is outside the scope of this volume, it is well worth learning more about it in some of the resources I recommend at the end of this book, particularly Bucher's memoir. It was a truly agonizing choice for Bucher, but he believed throughout the rest of his life that it was the right one.

What went through Bucher's mind during his fateful encounter with the North Korean navy? We have Bucher's own words to guide us. He gives a detailed account of his thought process in his autobiography, *Bucher: My Story*. Other members of his crew recounted events differently, including whether Bucher or his chief engineer made the decision to stop the *Pueblo*. Still, the book paints a vivid picture of a captain who desperately wanted to fight back but knew that it was not the most prudent course of action.

Bucher was in a vulnerable position. His mission required his vessel to drift while gathering signals intelligence. The *Pueblo* was by no means a fast ship, but the engagement started with it at a dead stop. In minutes, the situation shifted from a single inbound vessel to the *Pueblo* being surrounded. Being caught flat-footed took away much of Bucher's decision space.

Bucher also had his orders ringing in his ears: "Don't start a war." He might not have known that South Korea was calling for blood after the failed assassination attempt on President Park. But he still knew that the Cold War world was on edge with the ongoing war in Vietnam. The *Banner* had been harassed by the Soviets and the Chinese on its own missions, so the initial North Korean challenge did not come as a surprise—but Bucher's orders did not anticipate that the North Koreans would launch a direct attack in international waters.

There were two major priorities in Bucher's mind as the situation devolved and the shooting began: the lives of his crew and the safety of US national secrets. These two goals were not natural fits with each other. One of the courses of action that Bucher considered, scuttling the ship, would have put his crew's lives in danger. But the shallow waters removed that course from his list of options.

The decision to fight back was on the table but not practical. The *Pueblo* was a Navy ship, but it was not a true warship. By the time the *Pueblo*'s cover was blown, it was already surrounded by the North Koreans with guns trained on her position. Bucher's crew would not have survived long on the open deck without armor plating for the .50-caliber guns. Many would have died in the act of setting up the covered weapons, to say nothing of those who would have perished in a vicious firefight so far from friendly waters. Perhaps that decision could have been considered if it might have protected the national secrets on board. But the token resistance would not have slowed the North Korean assault. More likely, it would have accelerated it.

The casualties belowdecks weighed on Bucher's mind as well. Only when the injuries started to mount did Bucher's mindset begin to shift away from withdrawal and delay to surrender. The consequences were stark when Bucher ordered the *Pueblo* to stop for the second time and the crew sustained casualties.

Bucher's decision-making throughout was constrained by decisions made long before the *Pueblo* ever got close to North Korea. Because most of the crew were prohibited from the NSG spaces, they were unable to adequately train for or assist in destruction procedures. Destroying the equipment and documents took much longer than it needed to. This forced Bucher to find alternate ways to stall for time while being escorted into North Korean waters. This had tragic consequences for the crewman who died when Bucher gave the second order to stop the ship.

But Bucher's decisions before January 24 were not the only ones that mattered. The Navy's decision to scrimp on destruction equipment forced Bucher's hand in the heat of the moment. And the decision to label the risk of North Korean aggression as low despite numerous indications to the contrary left the *Pueblo* woefully unprepared when confronted by overwhelming force.

Another important thing to consider about Bucher's mindset is that there might have been help coming. The last message from Japan was that air assets could be on their way for relief. As a counterfactual, how would history have looked at Bucher had he gone out guns blazing and US aircraft arrived minutes later to find a sinking wreck? Dean Rusk, President Lyndon Johnson's secretary of state, was eager to call the *Pueblo* seizure an "act of war" when the crew was imprisoned and a single crewman lost his life. What would it have looked like if eighty-three sailors had perished instead? It does not take a strong imagination to envision a string of reprisals greatly increasing the risk of general war, as it did when North Korea shot down an American EC-121 surveillance plane in 1969.

What can we learn from Bucher's hard choice? First, context is important. John Paul Jones did secure an improbable victory over the HMS *Serapis* when all hope seemed lost. But while the *Bonhomme Richard* was inferior to the *Serapis*, it was at least also a true warship, not an oceanographic research vessel. It had comparable guns, was already in motion, and had a crew prepared for combat of that kind. Pete Bucher's situation was different in every way. The .50-caliber guns on the *Pueblo* could have given the North Korean torpedo boats trouble. But those guns were seriously outclassed by the sub chasers' automatic cannon. Jones's dedication to combat is worthy of emulation, but had he been in a dinghy instead of the *Bonhomme*, he would have sung a different tune. And there was no shame in eighteenth-century navies surrendering a command if truly overmatched—even Jack Aubrey of fictional fame does so in *Master and Commander*, and so did Stephen Decatur on one occasion, one of the great heroes of the US Navy.

This is something that leaders should remember: tradition for its own sake is not enough to justify a decision. Living up to the brave history of an organization is a worthy goal. But simply following tradition instead of carefully evaluating a situation can be a dangerous shortcut that may lead to bad decisions. In the military world, we remark that someone is "fighting the last war" when they use an old approach without adapting to new conditions. If we lean on analogies that connect an eighteenth-century sailing warship to a small, essentially unarmed spy ship 150 years later, we are in effect fighting that last proverbial war forever.

Choices need to be made on the merits of the moment, with an open and innovative mind. Pete Bucher did not make his choice out of cowardice; he made a painful cost-benefit calculation that resistance would waste lives and not protect the national secrets on his ship. Bucher's decision protected his crew and ultimately served the interests of the nation by destroying as much classified material as possible before the *Pueblo* was boarded—just as Bucher knew it would be when the North Koreans cut off all possible escape routes. After a great deal of thought, I've concluded that condemning eighty young men to die for the pride of the Navy would not have made him a hero; it would have made him a modern Captain Ahab, obsessed to the point of self-destruction. My old friend and mentor Vice Admiral Hal Bowen disagreed and saw it as a simple black-and-white choice. I do not.

The lessons of Bucher's decision echo in every category of human activity, military or otherwise. Relying on established practice is a comfortable thing to do. It simplifies decision-making and establishes a sense of order in a chaotic universe. Indeed, large organizations need structure refined over time by learning best practices. But leaving those traditions unexamined for a long time leads to ossified thinking. Organizations need to be in a constant state of keeping what works and removing what does not. Failing to do so is worse than laziness; it is an abdication of leadership.

It is also important to remember that a single hard choice is not made in a void. The lead-up to a crisis is just as important as decisions made within the crisis itself. The difficult thing here is that predicting a crisis is not an exact science. This is why it is crucial for all leaders to plan. Inevitably all plans will change; in the military we often say that "no plan survives first contact with the enemy." But the act of planning is what counts. By thinking through contingencies in advance, it is possible to better predict crisis scenarios and thus provide greater decision-making flexibility for leaders in a moment of crisis. It engenders a mental discipline for people who go into difficult situations, forcing them to think through how to react in different scenarios. It removes the most powerful constraint on those making hard choices: a lack of imagination. While I might have sympathy for Bucher's situation, the court of inquiry did the right thing by criticizing those senior to him in the chain of command—some of whom briefed Bucher while his ship was in Pearl Harbor on the voyage across the Pacific—and who downplayed the risk of North Korean aggression before the mission.

The title of this chapter is "No Way Out," and it, of course, refers to the attempts that Commander Bucher made to delay the seemingly inevitable after the North Koreans surrounded his crew and demanded its surrender. But "the delayer" was also the nickname of Quintus Fabius, the Roman general who led a long delaying strategy against Hannibal in the Italian Peninsula during the Second Punic War. Fabius's contemporaries claimed he was a coward and looked down on him at the time, but history bore out that it was the right strategy. This type of hard choice—between taking courageous but costly action as opposed to playing for time and seeking to live in order to fight another day—have been a part of naval and military history since mankind first went to war.

More recently another naval officer, one much younger than Bucher at the time of the *Pueblo* incident, faced a similar hard choice. In mid-January 2016, two Navy riverine boats were seized by the Iranian Revolutionary Guard Corps forces after they accidentally (through a combination of bad navigational equipment and carelessness) entered Iranian waters near Farsi Island in the Arabian Gulf. The two boats were on a routine passage in the Gulf with ten sailors divided between them. One of the boats had a mechanical problem, and while both boats were stopped to work on it, they drifted into Iranian waters. What happened next looked like the *Pueblo* incident—the Navy boats were surrounded by Iranian craft, with crew-served weapons armed, demanding the Americans surrender. The sailors were then forced to their knees with their hands behind their heads and held prisoner for the next fifteen hours.

Fortunately, at this time late in the Obama administration, the United States and Iran had a better relationship than is the case today. The then secretary of state John Kerry worked with his opposite number to secure the release of the sailors the next day. The lieutenant in charge of the two boats provided a video in which he thanked the Iranians for "fantastic" behavior and apologized profusely for entering their territorial waters. All of this stirred old memories of *Pueblo*.

The Iranians predictably celebrated the incident profusely, as you would expect, saying that many of the sailors cried during the brief period of detention and pointing out that this was a significant victory for Iran over the United States. The US Navy conducted an investigation and disciplined the senior leaders on the two boats as well as three officers at higher-echelon commands in the Gulf. While this incident was, thankfully, far less lengthy and brutal, the basic questions for the Navy remain: What is a commander's responsibility to resist surrender in the face of overwhelming odds against successfully fighting back? How far should the commander go in preserving the honor of the Navy in the face of deadly force?

As was the case for both Bucher and the lieutenant in the Gulf, the short answer is that it is a decision for the commander on the scene and in the moment. While we all like to think we would be John Paul Jones, every scenario is different. And the eighteenth-century Navy is rife with examples of highly respected captains who surrendered their swords when it was apparent they were about to lose a fight rather than allow an opponent to simply pour fire into their already burning hull and kill their crews. For me, the key is the phrase "means to resist." If there is still a sufficient possibility of turning the situation to advantage, or delaying until reinforcements can arrive, or bluffing an opponent into pausing, I would say: take the chance. But when there is literally nothing left in the locker of resistance tools—such as Bucher's case where his crew-served weapons were frozen under tarps, for example—then it is time to live to fight another day.

This book is titled *To Risk It All* for a reason. Bucher's hard choice was not to risk it all, but rather to attempt to save the lives of his crew. That choice would define the rest of his life and earn him the ire of good men like Vice Admiral Hal Bowen. But the right choice is not always the popular choice, and in my view Bucher made the hardest of the decisions examined in this volume with real courage and common sense. For anyone making a hard choice, it is wise to think through the balance between what may feel like the idealistic decision to continue, knowing you will fail, and taking the pragmatic way out. Evaluating the situation realistically, leaving aside the pressures of tradition and the voices we think we hear from the chorus of observers not in the arena, helps clarify the path forward. When there is simply no way out, that inner voice says: Make a pragmatic choice. As we say in North Florida where I am from, "Sometimes you gotta know the difference between quitting . . . and getting beat."

CHAPTER EIGHT

Pirates of the Gulf of Aden

———◆———

Rear Admiral Michelle Howard,
United States Navy

Commander, USS Boxer,
Combined Task Force 151

RESCUE OF CAPTAIN RICHARD
PHILLIPS FROM SOMALI PIRATES
IN THE INDIAN OCEAN

APRIL 12, 2009

This is not for wimps.[1]

One of the most difficult choices any military leader ever makes is the decision to attempt a hostage rescue. During my three years as commander of US Southern Command (SOUTHCOM) in Miami, Florida, from 2006 to 2009, I spent a great deal of time focused on trying to organize the rescue of three American hostages held in brutal jungle confinement by the Fuerzas Armadas Revolucionarias de Colombia (Revolutionary Armed Forces of Colombia, or FARC, the acronym in Spanish), a Marxist guerrilla organization. Marc Gonsalves, Keith Stansell, and Tom Howes were Northrop Grumman contractors working an intelligence contract for SOUTHCOM when they were captured after their small aircraft crashed in the Colombian jungle in 2003. They had spent three hellish years in captivity by the time I took command and—as had each of my predecessors—we made their rescue the number-one operational priority of the command. We had been working assiduously to locate them in their captivity and had US special forces ready to conduct a rescue at a moment's notice.[2]

But the more I looked at the odds of successfully rescuing them, the less enthusiastic I became about launching a bold commando raid. When you really dig into the statistics on special forces hostage-rescue attempts, they are not very encouraging—especially against highly motivated and well-armed terrorist groups. In well over half the cases, the hostages are killed or wounded. Normally, terrorist groups have well-rehearsed plans that involve killing the closely guarded hostages at the first sign of an attack. For the first couple of years that I was in command at SOUTHCOM, from 2006 to 2008, we had several good "looks" at the location of the hostages, but never a "clean shot," so to speak. I met with the hostages' families, and the sense I got from them was not to take any chances on a raid that would result in the deaths of the three men. I would have felt the same way if I were in their shoes.

Eventually, it was the Colombian military that came up with a brilliant scheme to essentially trick the FARC into turning the hostages over to what they thought was a humanitarian nongovernmental organization. The story of that rescue is quite extraordinary, but even that scheme—creative, subtle, and bold at once—was fraught with peril for the hostages and therefore a very difficult decision both on the Colombian and the US sides.[3] As one of the decision-makers in that raid, I hesitated until the last moment. Because the risks in hostage-rescue missions are so high, the tendency is always to wait a bit longer and hope for a mistake on the part of the terrorists that enables a less dangerous mission. Eventually, I briefed the plan to the National Security Council, and the president personally gave the green light. When I finished the brief in the Situation Room, I was a very nervous four-star—but had all the pieces in place to proceed.

As I mentioned in the introduction, I've often felt in decision-making that a leader cannot allow a desire for "perfect" to defeat a "very good" potential solution, but in the case of hostage rescue, you really need a near-perfect set of circumstances before pulling the figurative trigger. As a result, I may have waited too long for the perfect shot at a rescue for Marc, Keith, and Tom. But eventually we supported the Colombian plan and succeeded in bringing our three Americans home alive. The most rewarding moment of my three years in command at US Southern Command was a barbecue we held for Marc, Keith, and Tom at our Miami headquarters after their rescue and release. Many of us wept that day to see them home at last.[4]

Which brings us to Admiral Michelle J. Howard, a pioneering officer who at the one-star level in her career had to make that most difficult of decisions: literally and figuratively pulling the trigger on a hostage rescue in a scenario that seemed stacked against the hostage. This is the story of Captain Richard Phillips, the *Maersk Alabama*, Somali pirates, and the courage it takes not only to pull the trigger but to delegate to the on-scene commander the authority to do so.

I met Michelle J. Howard when she was a midshipman at the US Naval Academy in the early 1980s, and even then, she was considered someone to watch. Over the thirty-six years of her career, I was proud to be among those who mentored her and watched her steady progression. She became the first African American woman to command a US warship, and went on to be the first to wear the four stars of a full admiral. During the *Maersk Alabama* mission, she faced the classic perils that any commander does in making the decision to execute a combat rescue—limited time, enormous risk, and the real possibility of losing a hostage in an instant. As I did when considering the hostage-rescue mission in Colombia, the then rear admiral Howard had to weigh her desire for a perfect operation against the known risks and the inherent uncertainties of delegating authority for quick and decisive action. How she made that very difficult choice—which turned out well, obviously, something you know if you've seen the excellent Tom Hanks film *Captain Phillips*—is a story worth examining in detail.

Michelle Howard was born on April 30, 1960, to Nick and Philippa Howard. She was immersed in the military life early: her father was a master sergeant in the Air Force and as is typical for active duty military, the family moved around the United States a great deal during her childhood. Her earliest years were spent at March Air Force Base in Southern California, but she graduated from high school in Aurora, Colorado. Along the way, she set her sights on a military career of her own. Though she was initially unsure which branch of service she would pursue, a television program crystallized her interest in the Naval Academy. Her mother then had the difficult task of telling her daughter that women were not allowed to attend Annapolis yet, but she also said that the family would sue if the policy had not changed by the time Michelle reached college age. She strongly considered the Air Force Academy as well as Annapolis. Happily, the exclusion was lifted before it came to lawsuits, and the Navy won out over the Air Force. Howard headed east to begin her studies at the Naval Academy in the summer of 1978.

This was a courageous and pioneering decision in its own right. The Academy had opened its gates to women only two years before, and the entire service was still roiled by Admiral Elmo Zumwalt's attempts in the early 1970s to force a reckoning with the dismal state of race and gender relations in the Navy.[5] Women were also barred from serving in ships or aircraft that might see combat—which, Howard knew, would make it that much harder for women to earn the full respect and highest promotions of a warfighting service. Although the female exclusion policy from combat operations would largely remain in force until 1993, Howard volunteered for sea duty immediately upon graduating in 1982. She was assigned first aboard the submarine tender USS *Hunley* and then the training carrier USS *Lexington*—though highly modified, the same *Lexington* that had sailed with Admiral Halsey in the climactic battles of the war in the Pacific, including Leyte Gulf. Howard's courage and skill were recognized early, and she quickly earned respect. In 1987, just five years out of the Academy, she received the Captain Winifred Collins Award for outstanding leadership—granted to just one woman officer each year selected from the entire US Navy—in recognition of her service aboard the *Lexington*.

Howard's leadership and decision-making style were forged in the often unforgiving climate of the Navy of that era. Reflecting on her career in 2010, she said, "Like the pioneering women of old, you have to let some things go."[6] Still, that did not mean letting *everything* go—and Howard knew when and where to draw the line. During her *Lexington* tour in the mid-1980s, some fellow female officers complained to Howard about a male captain's unacceptable behavior, and she decided to confront him, knowing that she was risking her career by doing so. "[I]f I didn't have the courage to talk to the captain," Howard recalled in 2017, "how will I ever have the courage to lead sailors into battle?"[7] Luckily, in this instance, the captain agreed to change his behavior. Smart man.

Howard's tireless pursuit of excellence continued through the 1990s. She spent most of the decade at sea, earning positions of increasing responsibility and serving in conflict zones both before and after women were officially allowed to sail into combat. Howard was assigned as chief engineer of the ammunition ship USS *Mount Hood* in the Gulf War of 1991, and then as first lieutenant of *Mount Hood*'s sister ship *Flint* from 1992. Within four years, she was promoted to executive officer of the dock landing ship USS *Tortuga*, which served back-to-back deployments first in support of the peacekeeping mission in the former Yugoslavia and then in training with several African navies. As the decade drew to a close, Howard achieved a milestone on March 12, 1999, when she became the first African American woman to command a US Navy ship: *Tortuga*'s sister USS *Rushmore*.

Following her command tour, Howard spent much of the 2000s ashore in planning and operations roles on the Joint and Navy staffs in the Pentagon. Those roles—which are crucial stepping-stones for officers on their way to flag rank—were interspersed with further command at sea. For about a year and a half between 2004 and 2005, Howard took charge of Amphibious Squadron 7, which participated in relief efforts following the devastating tsunami in Indonesia.

The then captain Howard returned ashore in late 2005 to take on a number of high-level strategy and policy jobs on the Navy staff and in the office of the secretary of the Navy. After two years serving as the senior military advisor in the secretary's office (a job I had held 1999–2001 and was proud to see Michelle take on), it was time for her to go back to sea. Like me a decade earlier, she was selected to one-star rear admiral at the end of her tour in the secretary of the Navy's office, and she received orders to take command of the Navy's Expeditionary Strike Group 2 and the international anti-piracy Combined Task Force 151. She was piped aboard her flagship, USS *Boxer*, in the first days of April 2009 and took up station off of "Pirate Alley," the mouth of the Gulf of Aden near Somalia. Little could she know that, within a week, four Somali teenagers would be the first pirates to capture a US-flagged ship in over a century and a half, and that, as on-scene commander of a high-stakes rescue mission, she would spend five sleepless days and nights pulling all the levers of her new command—and then some—to extricate Captain Richard Phillips from his high-profile plight.

In the first decade of the twenty-first century, many Americans were surprised to learn that pirates were not totally consigned to the fictional seas of the popular Disney ride "Pirates of the Caribbean" or the popular Captain Jack Sparrow movies. Piracy had not been a front-page problem since Stephen Decatur's day in the early nineteenth century, but a new "pirate coast" along the Horn of Africa, just off the shores of Somalia, was beginning to attract attention. The rich cargoes of international shipping that passed near the coast proved a tempting target, and a frighteningly effective industry grew up to make prizes of the ships steaming by.

Virtually all countries deplore piracy as a form of criminal activity, but enforcement can be complicated in situations where capability does not match jurisdiction. Increasing piracy off the Somali coast led the European Union to start its first joint naval activity, Operation Atalanta, in December 2008. The US Navy contributed a task force, too—but with no American ships captured, we were not yet in the thick of the action when Michelle Howard arrived to take command as a one-star rear admiral at the beginning of April 2009. That same week, however, the US-flagged container ship *Maersk Alabama* would set out on an ill-fated voyage from Oman to Kenya, by way of Pirate Alley off the horn of Somalia.

The ship was commanded by Captain Richard Phillips and carried a crew of twenty-three, plus a nineteen-thousand-ton cargo of humanitarian supplies. All aboard knew they were sailing through dangerous waters; Captain Phillips ran the ship and crew through anti-piracy drills on April 7, the day before their ordeal began. Meanwhile, aboard the amphibious assault ship USS *Boxer*, Admiral Howard was still adjusting to the rigors and rhythms of her new role in command of the anti-piracy task force. As the sun set on April 7, neither could know how dramatically their circumstances would shift in the next twenty-four hours: by nightfall on the eighth, Captain Phillips would be a hostage aboard his own ship's lifeboat, while Admiral Howard would be in contact with the president and organizing every US naval asset in the area—and additional forces from the Arabian Gulf—in a race against time to save Captain Phillips.

Around midnight, as April 7 turned into April 8, the *Maersk Alabama*'s lookouts spotted a small pirate skiff dogging the cargo ship from several miles away. The sailors took evasive action throughout the rest of the night but could not shake the interlopers. The eighth dawned clear and calm—perfect conditions for the pirates. By 7:15 a.m., the pirates had come within a mile of their intended prize, and Captain Phillips rang the alarm. With horns blaring throughout the ship, the crew sprang into action—showering the approaching pirates with water from the on-deck sprinklers, swinging the ship's rudder to try to sink the tiny pirate skiff as it approached, and securing themselves inside a specially fortified compartment belowdecks as the pirates came ever closer to the ship.

For about forty-five tense minutes, the *Maersk Alabama*'s crew put their training to work with all the urgency of a real-world crisis. But the pirates were able to pull alongside the cargo ship, and one of them managed to clamber over the rail. By swinging the rudder, the American crew was creating waves that threatened to sink the pirate skiff, but the one pirate already aboard leveled his rifle at a couple of sailors and forced them to lower a ladder to the other three pirates. Those three scrambled up as their skiff sank beneath them, at once becoming the first pirates to capture a US-flagged ship since the 1820s and completely stranded aboard their prize.

By a little after 8:00 a.m., the crew had cut all the ship's power and taken control away from the bridge. Most had secured themselves in the reinforced compartment, which was pitch-dark and fast becoming unbearably hot. (Many, too, were hungry: breakfast had been prepared but not served when the alarm rang.) The pirates were holding Captain Phillips and several crewmen hostage on the bridge, while a couple of officers stayed mobile, listening to the captain on their two-way radios while dodging pirates in the dark gangways of the ship.

Events moved quickly through the rest of that day, April 8 —if hellishly for the crew barricaded, sweating, and thirsting belowdecks. Aboard the *Maersk Alabama*, one of the ship's mates captured the leader of the pirates, and a couple of the sailors initially trapped with Captain Phillips managed to slip away. By midafternoon, the leaderless pirates were looking for a way off the ship—and Captain Phillips had helped them devise a plan to use the lifeboat. The captain radioed his crew to restore the ship's power and prepare to exchange the captured pirate for himself and the last crew members still held hostage. After about an hour of preparations, all was ready: the crew released the pirate, the pirates released the hostage crewmen, and everyone prepared to lower the lifeboat. But the four pirates, reneging on their agreement, took Captain Phillips with them as they climbed into the tiny orange craft. Nevertheless, by 5:00 p.m., the *Maersk Alabama* was secure. Her crew breathed fresh air on deck while her captain and his four captors bobbed along in the lifeboat astern.

Meanwhile, the US Navy was mounting a response to the unfolding crisis. Two warships, the destroyer USS *Bainbridge* and the frigate USS *Halyburton*, steamed to rendezvous with the *Maersk Alabama* in the Gulf of Aden. After an overnight transit, they arrived on scene early in the morning of April 9. *Bainbridge* and *Halyburton* took up station a few hundred yards away (out of rifle range) from the lifeboat containing the pirates and their hostage, Captain Phillips. *Bainbridge* deployed her small unmanned aerial vehicle to get an overhead view of the situation and established radio contact with the pirates—both to ascertain Captain Phillips's condition and to open negotiations. With the Navy in control of the situation, the *Maersk Alabama* made ready to continue on to her original destination of Mombasa, Kenya, with an armed security team aboard to ensure the rest of the voyage went smoothly.

Friday, April 10, was a day of on-site negotiations and global mobilization. Rear Admiral Howard, as commanding officer of the US Navy's regional anti-piracy task force, sailed to rendezvous with *Bainbridge* and *Halyburton* aboard her flagship, the large-deck amphibious carrier USS *Boxer*. A team of SEAL snipers flew to the scene from their base in

Virginia, parachuting into the ocean and swimming over to the *Bainbridge*, where they set up shooting positions. And the Navy's senior commanders asked for and received standing authorization to use deadly force if Captain Phillips's life was deemed to be in imminent danger. As a practical matter, that authority was Admiral Howard's to exercise, and she delegated the decision to authorize the snipers to actually fire to Commander Frank Castellano, commanding officer of the *Bainbridge*.

From the night of the tenth through the eleventh, tensions ratcheted up. After night fell on Friday, Captain Phillips tried to rescue himself by jumping out of the lifeboat. The pirates fired into the water around him and quickly brought him back aboard—then dumped the radios they had received from the Navy into the water for fear that the negotiators were somehow secretly communicating with their captive. All Saturday, the seas worsened, tossing the tiny lifeboat around; by 5:00 p.m., the crew of the *Bainbridge* convinced the seasick pirates to accept a towline, theoretically to keep the small craft more stable in the destroyer's wake. This also had the advantage of keeping the pirates from reaching shore—and of controlling the range, should the SEALs need to shoot. As the hours stretched on, the *Bainbridge* slowly but surely reeled in the lifeboat to about thirty yards.

Rear Admiral Howard had been up for forty-eight hours and was closely monitoring the ongoing situation from her command center. For a commander, this is often the hardest place to be: effectively on-scene by virtue of instantaneous communications, but one layer back from the actual point of "batteries released." I have been there on several occasions, and it is decidedly uncomfortable, leading to second-guessing about everything from the reliability of the radio communications to the steadiness of the sailors at the point of the spear. As Saturday turned into Sunday, Michelle Howard felt events were coming to a head. It took every bit of the patience and steadiness honed in a long career at sea to let the situation develop. In the Navy, we say in ship handling that sometimes the hardest thing to do after applying engine and rudder commands to the vessel is simply to stop and see what effect they are having. I have often seen junior officers continue to pile on commands, and the ship never has a chance to catch up, leaving the ship driver in a precarious downward spiral. Michelle stayed steady as risk compounded, remaining with the plan she'd put together two days earlier, and knowing that a culminating point was looming.

By Sunday the twelfth, tensions aboard the lifeboat were nearing the breaking point: the pirates had been in the operation for the better part of five days, and there were no toilets or other creature comforts on the cramped craft. In midafternoon, the lead pirate—the same one who had been captured by the *Maersk Alabama*'s crew—radioed the *Bainbridge* to request medical assistance and offer to negotiate. US sailors brought him over to the destroyer in a small boat of their own. Without their leader, the other three pirates grew more panicky, and around 6:00 p.m., there was a scuffle aboard the lifeboat. Spotters aboard the *Bainbridge* saw a pirate leveling a rifle at Captain Phillips's back, and Commander Castellano authorized the SEALs to shoot. Minutes later, the snipers had clear sight pictures on all three pirates aboard the lifeboat. Three shots rang out as one, and the three pirates dropped from view. A SEAL slid down the towline, ensured the pirates were dead, and whisked Captain Phillips off the lifeboat. He was evacuated into the destroyer for a medical checkup, a change of clothes, and an intelligence debriefing aboard the *Boxer*.[8] Howard's plan—full of risk—had worked.

In the end, the rescue was what SEALs call a "perfect op": everything went exactly as they had trained, planned, and hoped. Despite the best training and preparation, reality rarely allows for perfection—which makes Admiral Howard's role in the crisis all the more striking.

It is one thing to make a hard choice knowing you will live with the consequences of your own actions. But it is another to make a hard choice that depends on someone else's actions. Unlike Stephen Decatur, Admiral Howard was not going to defeat the pirates with her own hand—instead, she had to decide what to do with the life-and-death authority given to her by the president, knowing that the situation was playing out under the unblinking scrutiny of the international media. At the time of the rescue, she had been aboard USS *Boxer* and in command of the task force for only a week; even as she was learning the ropes in her new role, she was responsible for commanding and coordinating all the new assets suddenly on-scene, from aircraft to SEALs. "That's an eye-opening way to start a new job," she quipped later. "Synchronizing that kind of might and capability was pretty amazing."[9]

In order to do her job effectively, she had to let everyone else do theirs—doubly difficult in the complex, stressful, and high-stakes setting of a hostage crisis. Once the president authorized the use of lethal force, responsibility fell to her as the senior commander on the scene to decide when and how to apply the force at her disposal.

By authorizing the SEALs to shoot, she was delegating that authority at least two levels down—to Commander Castellano, who, with eyes on the lifeboat, would judge the threat to the captain, and to the SEAL snipers, whose split-second execution would result in either a "perfect op" or the devasting loss of a hostage and deep public embarrassment. In the long tradition of command at sea, Admiral Howard knew full well she would be responsible for an outcome she could not directly control. Though new to her command, she applied her training, knowledge, and experience to the situation. But there was also a very personal component to her decision. That she made the decision so quickly and effectively in a case where perfection was needed within days or hours of the incident unfolding—not, for example, waiting the months that I'd wrestled with the Colombian hostage situation at SOUTHCOM—is a testament both to her personal fortitude and the highest traditions of the Navy as well.

Small wonder, then, that this pioneering woman would go on, in succeeding years, to shatter still more barriers and ascend to the very highest rank. A little more than a year after the Captain Phillips rescue, in August 2010, she became the first Black woman promoted to two-star rear admiral. Two years later, she pinned on the third star of a vice admiral, and on July 1, 2014, she became the first female four-star admiral and the first woman to serve as vice chief of naval operations—the second-highest position in the US Navy. In 2016, she moved from the Pentagon to take command of all US naval forces in Europe and Africa, becoming the first four-star woman admiral to serve in such a role. This remarkable leader retired from active duty on December 1, 2017, and has continued her service in academia and the private sector since then.

Admiral Howard is an inspiring example with her thirty-five-year voyage in the Navy, and her decisions and actions in the crucible of the *Maersk Alabama* crisis offer some especially pertinent lessons for today's leaders. Whereas Stephen Decatur's actions against the Barbary pirates were an example of individual bravery, Admiral Howard's experience more closely mirrored that of a modern executive: faced with a complex and fast-moving crisis only a week into her role, she had ninety-six hours in the global media spotlight to coordinate the resources under her command and validate the responsibility entrusted to her from above.

The first lesson to draw from Admiral Howard's example is the importance of entrusting decisions to the people who need to make them. As the senior officer managing the crisis, her job was to conduct the orchestra rather than to play the instruments. Over the five days of the crisis, she was given steadily more resources and more responsibility, and she had to determine how to employ both. Once the SEALs arrived, she had both the means and the authority to use lethal force if Captain Phillips's life was in immediate danger—yet, without her own finger on the trigger or her own eyes on the lifeboat, she quickly and correctly delegated tactical control of the snipers to Commander Castellano on the *Bainbridge*. Knowing that imminent danger would not allow time for a radio relay from the SEALs to Commander Castellano to her and back, she entrusted the people in position to make the decision to do so, knowing that she would bear ultimate responsibility for the outcome. Too often as the "decider in chief," we hesitate to delegate the really significant authorities. Michelle's story is a pretty good example of getting it right.

Second, Admiral Howard deserves a lot of credit for not seeking the credit. In the blockbuster *Captain Phillips* movie, she "appears" only as a voice over the radio. She bore full responsibility for what transpired on-scene, and the world likely would have heard a lot about Michelle Howard if the rescue attempt had been any less perfectly executed—and she would almost certainly not have gone on to serve as vice chief of naval operations or the first woman admiral in charge of combatant forces. The lopsided risks of appearing before the klieg lights of the always-on global media constitute a minefield that modern decision-makers must learn to navigate effectively. They have to balance their roles in an organizational hierarchy with the intense glare of public scrutiny. Admiral Howard not only passed this test with flying colors but—with rare and admirable humility—did not indulge any subsequent desire to be puffed up as the hero of the day. The lesson for all of us as decision-makers here is straightforward—we should not base our call on fear or favor. Easy to say, hard to do; and Michelle Howard took the right approach in her hard decision.

Finally, Admiral Howard's actions—not only during the *Maersk Alabama* crisis but throughout her career—are a powerful reminder that great responsibility can be thrust upon us at any moment, and that exceptional leaders are perfectly capable of rising to the occasion—even if it is something they have not contemplated or planned. Although she had been sent to command an anti-piracy task force, there was no way of predicting that pirates would capture a US-flagged ship for the first time in over two centuries in Admiral Howard's first week on the job. Nevertheless, she responded to an unexpected crisis with great courage, inner confidence, and unshakable professionalism when circumstances demanded. Having carried the burdens and pressure of a pioneer throughout her service, Admiral Howard demonstrated that her decision-making fortitude more than justified the Navy's faith in her ability—and paved the way for succeeding generations of leaders who better represent the talent and diversity of today's United States.

Her decision-making skills are the ones the Navy seeks to inculcate in our commanders as they work their way up the long chain of command. Drawing on both her own inner sense of judgment as well as the recommendations of her subordinates, she was able to delegate even in the most challenging and risky of circumstances. That nicely balanced set of attributes, coupled with her groundbreaking ascent as a Black woman officer, will remain a vibrant legacy for the Navy as it moves forward in the challenging seas of the twenty-first century.

CHAPTER NINE

The Red Flare

Captain Brett Crozier, United States Navy

Commanding Officer, USS
Theodore Roosevelt *(CVN-71)*

DEALING WITH A DEADLY COVID
OUTBREAK IN *ROOSEVELT*

MARCH 30, 2020

We are not at war. Sailors do not need to die. If we
do not act now, we are failing to properly take care
of our most trusted asset—our Sailors.[1]

I first came to know Captain Brett "Chopper" Crozier when he was part of my team at US European Command/NATO during the Libyan intervention in 2011. He played a vital role as one of our targeting operators (called a "targeteer") on board the Strike Force NATO flagship, USS *Mount Whitney*. This was during the final days of Operation Odyssey Dawn, the US set of strikes that preceded the NATO mission. When I was asked to take over the mission in my NATO role as Supreme Allied Commander, I pulled Crozier over to the NATO joint task force, which was operating out of Naples. The NATO mission was called Operation Unified Protector (although frankly it was hardly "unified," with many of the NATO allies declining to participate). On the Unified Protector team, Crozier worked for a brilliant Canadian three-star aviator, Lieutenant General

Charlie Bouchard. All of Captain Crozier's bosses found him a talented and quite extraordinary officer.

His job in both the early (and brief) US mission Operation Odyssey Dawn and the longer and much more complex NATO Operation Unified Protector mission was the most important and delicate on the team: the selection, evaluation, and vetting of air-strike targets. NATO had been given the overall Libyan mission by the United Nations, and we had one important restriction: we were not permitted to put boots on the ground. Despite that restriction, we had to 1) conduct an arms embargo on both air and sea to prevent Libya's then strongman Muammar Gaddafi from obtaining any further arms or ammunition, 2) establish a countrywide no-fly zone to prevent Gaddafi from using his airpower against the rebels, and 3) stop Gaddafi from using his land power (which was extensive and brutal) against the people of Libya. Clearly it was going to be an airpower-heavy operation.

All this raised delicate questions over the rules of engagement and required us to use precision-guided air-to-ground strikes without causing any collateral damage to innocent civilians. For a target selector, this presents a very constrained set of choices. For example, Crozier would have to evaluate the military value of the target (could he definitively show that it was linked to threats against the people of Libya?). He also had to show his chain of command—up to the four-star admiral in Naples, Admiral Sam Locklear, my direct subordinate—that there was close to zero chance of any harm befalling innocent civilians. And finally, Crozier had to evaluate the best aircraft and weapons system to put against the target (Tomahawk missiles, fighter aircraft with precision-guided munitions, helicopters with short-range missiles, etc.). Everything he did was closely scrutinized not only by the military chain of command but by the media broadly. And all of it unfolded under relentless international pressure from the twenty-eight nations of NATO—some of which, like Germany, were simply opposed to NATO's involvement in the Libyan campaign entirely.

In the end, Crozier and his team planned and executed 218 air tasking orders (ATOs), mammoth action orders that plan out the complex movements of aircraft in combat zones. NATO aircraft flew over 26,500 flights, including 9,700 that attacked ground targets and destroyed over 5,900 military assets, all while deconflicting operations with over 6,700 humanitarian aid flights and ground movements. And they did all this with the lowest level of collateral damage in the history of air operations.[2] It was a stunningly successful military campaign, and Crozier's part in it was rewarded with two significant medals: one from NATO and one from the United States. I thought then that he'd surely go on to an admiral's stars, and over the next several years I watched his steady progress toward that goal: nuclear power school, command at sea of a deep-draft warship, duty as the executive officer of a nuclear carrier, and finally command of the prestigious nuclear aircraft carrier USS *Theodore Roosevelt*. By October 2019, when I was speaking at a dinner of the Theodore Roosevelt Association and ran into some representatives from the ship, I learned that he would soon be deploying forward to the Western Pacific and probably the Arabian Gulf as captain in *Roosevelt*. I had little doubt he'd become a one-star admiral within a year or so.

Thus, I was stunned to see the outbreak of COVID-19 in his ship following a chain of command–directed port visit to Vietnam, an unexpected and dramatic turn of events that placed him in an unenviable and unprecedented position. With the virus running rampant through his carrier's five-thousand-person crew, he worked diligently with his chain of command in the Pacific Fleet to find some way to get the carrier off-line safely, heal his crew, and get the ship back to fighting capability as quickly as possible.

All this was happening largely below the level of public scrutiny until, in frustration over lack of effective solutions, Crozier wrote an email to his chain of command and chose to send it over an unclassified circuit, instead of more prudently using classified means to transmit it. It was the ultimate "red flare,"* calling for help. Unfortunately, the email leaked and created a firestorm of criticism directed toward his Navy chain of command and ultimately toward his own leadership in the crisis. The acting secretary of the Navy, Thomas Modly, personally relieved him of duty as the ship's captain, and then flew from Washington to Guam to deliver an ill-advised and profanity-laced oration to the crew (who loved their captain and correctly viewed Crozier's efforts as stemming entirely from his desire to care for them). The video of Captain Crozier departing his ship in Guam for the last time and being cheered by the entire crew is deeply moving.

The incident will be studied for decades in Navy leadership classes and especially in sessions preparing officers for command at sea. At the time he sent that red-flare email, Brett Crozier was tired, frustrated, and dealing with a chain of command that offered a confusing and poorly orchestrated set of solutions. In retrospect, he should have sent it via a classified network. He failed to include as recipients all the right individuals in his chain of command (in particular, leaving out the important three-star commander of the Western Pacific's Seventh Fleet). But there is no doubt that Crozier wrote it from his heart, was pleading for help from

---

* A "red flare" is naval slang for "a call for help," taken from shooting a flare at sea to signal distress to nearby ships.

the Navy chain of command, and felt he had to launch it to save the lives of his sailors.

He must have known his career would suffer terribly and probably fatally—and it did, resulting in his "relief for cause" (the Navy's version of firing someone in command) and effectively blocking him from selection to rear admiral. He had to know that was the overwhelmingly probable outcome of launching such a message. Yet he chose to put the welfare of his crew above his own career ambitions, precisely what the Navy would want of our sea captains. It was a hard choice indeed, and by examining how he went about making it, there are some powerful lessons to be drawn from the voyage of "Chopper" Crozier.

Brett Crozier was born on February 24, 1970, in Santa Rosa, California. He was sixteen years old when Paramount Pictures released the film that would inspire a generation of would-be flyers: *Top Gun*. Young Brett was instantly hooked and knew that he wanted to pilot jets himself.[3] He secured a nomination to the Naval Academy through then representative Douglas Bosco and graduated with the class of 1992. He reported to flight training in Florida after graduation and earned his wings in 1994.

Only his dream had a twist. Crozier was on track to be a naval aviator but not a jet pilot. Instead, he was sent to Hawaii as a pilot for SH-60B Seahawk helicopters. The Seahawk is a workhorse rotary-wing aircraft that can do a variety of missions, such as search and rescue, anti-submarine warfare, and resupply. It is a vital aircraft for the Navy and one that naval aviators by and large are proud to fly. But Crozier wanted to fly jet fighters and would not be deterred from fulfilling his dream. After completing a few years in the Arabian Gulf, Crozier was given a plum assignment in the Navy's personnel office. If he continued to perform well, then he would be able to write his ticket to anywhere in the Navy. He did just that and secured what he wanted: a slot in aircraft transition training to fly the F/A-18 Hornet. He earned the nickname "Chopper," both as a mocking taunt of the helicopters he had previously flown and a sign of respect for making an almost unheard-of transition.*

Throughout his Navy career, Crozier received accolades from both supervisors and peers. But unlike the archetypes of naval aviators portrayed in *Top Gun*, he was consistently credited as a humble team player. In the words of one of his roommates in flight training, "This is the last guy to go and seek attention. He's not a glory hound—not that guy."[4]

---

* The friendly rivalry between jet pilots and helicopter pilots is intense and will continue as long as both aircraft remain in the US military's inventory.

Crozier had a gift for supporting others while still pursuing his own ambitions for his life and career.

In 2003, while assigned to the strike fighter squadron VFA-94 (the "Mighty Shrikes"), he flew combat missions in Iraq from USS *Nimitz*. Subsequent to that assignment, his career began to accelerate. He was tapped for a series of top assignments that put him on the path to command, notably becoming an instructor pilot and getting a master's degree from the Naval War College. He came back to the Mighty Shrikes as their commander and saw them through combat operations in the Middle East. In 2010, he was sent to NATO, where I saw him excel firsthand, as described above.

He then ascended to the realm of commanding large vessels, a required stint for aviators seeking command of an aircraft carrier. After completing Naval Nuclear Power training, the gatekeeping course for those wanting to command carriers, Crozier became the executive officer (second in command) of the USS *Ronald Reagan*. He then became the commanding officer of the USS *Blue Ridge*, an amphibious command ship that serves as the flagship of the Seventh Fleet.* He served there until assuming his fateful

---

* Seventh Fleet is the numbered Navy fleet responsible for all Navy ships in the Indo-Pacific. Due to the winds of geopolitics, it is one of the most important parts of the Navy today. Crozier's selection for duty on the *Blue Ridge* was a clear demonstration of the esteem held by the Navy's leadership.

command of the USS *Theodore Roosevelt* on November 1, 2019.

Unbeknownst to Crozier, events were beginning to unfold that would define (and shorten) the rest of his career. On December 31, 2019, Americans were getting ready to ring in the New Year. On the same day on the other side of the Pacific, health officials in the Chinese city of Wuhan announced an outbreak of a new type of "pneumonia." Two weeks later, on January 17, the *Roosevelt* began its scheduled deployment to Asia. In China, Lunar New Year celebrations continued through January 25, helping to spread the coronavirus across the country and starting its steady expansion around the world. During this time, basic information about the virus was very limited. Human transmission was only being investigated around the Lunar New Year, and it would take months before it would be truly understood.

On February 7, the *Roosevelt* made its first visit to the island of Guam, a strategic US territory between Japan, the Philippines, and New Guinea. The carrier was then sent west and made a scheduled port visit to Da Nang, Vietnam, on March 5 at the request of the commander of the Pacific Fleet. The visit was scheduled as a "show the flag" visit to deepen the growing strategic relationship between the United States and the Vietnamese. At that point in early 2020, Vietnam had not experienced any major outbreaks.

But during the port visit, thirty-nine sailors were exposed to two British citizens staying at the same hotel who later tested positive for COVID-19. Those sailors were all quarantined in the rear of the ship to keep any infection from spreading further.

On March 11, the World Health Organization officially declared COVID-19 a worldwide pandemic. On Friday, March 13, the US government declared COVID a national emergency. Federal employees (like so many others) were told to work from home, effective immediately. The Department of Defense went into "stop movement," which barred all movement for routine job changes or work travel. Anything that was not related to combat operations ground to a halt. Guam, too, experienced its own set of outbreaks and declared a public emergency on March 14. One senior naval aviator wryly noted: "Fly safe, wash your hands, no high-fives."[5]

On March 24, three sailors aboard *Roosevelt* who had not been exposed to the thirty-nine quarantined crew members reported to the medical department that they had lost their senses of taste and smell.[6] Though these symptoms are now widely connected with COVID, few people then understood the various ways COVID can present. Those sailors did not have fevers or coughs, so they were sent back to work. Without tests or a nuanced understanding of how COVID spread, it would be easy to assume that they were suffering from any number of other illnesses that thrive in enclosed environments.

The crew's situation continued to spiral downward from there. Crozier's "decent sleep schedule" of four to five hours per night was gone, and his own level of exhaustion began to increase.[7] On March 26, the number of COVID cases jumped again, marking the start of the exponential spread of the virus on the *Roosevelt*. To get things back under control, the *Roosevelt* was routed back to Guam to move infected crew members off the ship more quickly and preserve the ship's ability to fight. The carrier arrived back in Guam on March 27. With enlisted sailors packed into cramped berthing compartments (more than a dozen sailors can bunk in a space the size of a typical suburban kitchen), the idea of social distancing was simply impossible.

Throughout this period, Captain Crozier was in more or less constant communication with a variety of levels in his chain of command. Much of the guidance he received, understandably enough, was muddled or contradictory—the entire Navy was trying to deal with a significant health crisis unlike anything in the past and operating on extremely limited scientific information. By March 28, the debate between Crozier, Seventh Fleet, and Navy headquarters both in Pearl Harbor and the Pentagon raged. New plans were being proposed and beaten back as new constraints were discovered. A scheme to airlift infected crew members all the way to hotel rooms in Okinawa was not logistically possible. The Navy made empty gyms and warehouses equipped with rudimentary cots available onshore in Guam days before. But Crozier and his leadership team resisted putting the sailors in those facilities; though the cots were intended to be spaced out six feet, the ship's medical officer believed that they were ineffective at actually keeping the virus under control. In addition, the crew was aware that the accommodations had limited access to food, internet, and phone service.[8] Word made it to leadership that many crew members might lie about their symptoms in order to stay on the *Roosevelt* during an active pandemic outbreak.[9] Meanwhile, the number of infected crew members rose again, and outbreaks were being reported within the ranks of sailors who had previously tested negative and had been put ashore.[10]

On March 29, Crozier and his leadership team decided to release the sailors held in aft quarantine. The number of people had steadily ballooned from the thirty-nine contacts identified in Vietnam to the thousand now held. This decision would later prove controversial, both because Crozier's chain of command was cut out of the loop and because it flew in the face of the most reliable method of controlling the spread of COVID. But keeping 20 percent of the ship's crew in close quarters also raised the risk of spread within that group, to say nothing of the logistical challenges of getting them food and other amenities. Worse still, the virus continued to spread throughout the main part of the ship. Crozier and his team judged that spreading those thousand people around the larger areas of the ship would be better for social distancing.[11] This proved to be a miscalculation.

Crozier remained convinced that individual hotel rooms was the only way to reliably stop the spread of the virus, identify which members were sick, and eventually get the ship back into fighting condition. There are many hotels in Guam (normally catering to Japanese tourists), but understandably the governor and the hotel industry resisted the idea of turning them over to the Navy, even on a paying basis. Releasing thousands of potentially infected crew members ran the risk of causing a mass outbreak on the island, of course, which local authorities naturally resisted. In the meantime, parts of Crozier's chain of command were getting into extended discussions about arcane technical issues such as whether to use Social Security numbers or Department of Defense ID numbers on testing kits.[12] He was not receiving steady, consistent guidance, and felt the situation was spinning out of control, with potentially deadly consequences for his crew.

On March 30, Crozier made his fateful decision to send up a red-flare email to try to short-circuit the bureaucracy and get access to private hotel rooms on Guam. The subject of the email and attached letter read (in all caps): REQUEST FOR ASSISTANCE IN RESPONSE TO COVID-19 PANDEMIC. Attached was a four-page-long letter that laid out, in crisp military staff writing style, the situation facing the *Roosevelt* and the rationale for needing individual rooms to get the COVID outbreak under control.[13]

The flare went up to the admirals in Crozier's chain of command, many of whom he knew personally from his time as a naval aviator, in the hopes that they could break the perceived logjam that kept the *Roosevelt*'s crew trapped. Crucially, Vice Admiral Bill Merz, a submariner and senior figure in Crozier's chain of command at Seventh Fleet, was left off the email, perhaps in an effort to get around bureaucratic hurdles that Crozier perceived existed on the Seventh Fleet staff. Crozier later regretted this move.[14] Unbeknownst to Crozier, the governor of Guam (under pressure from the Navy) had agreed to the hotel-room plan six hours before Crozier sent his email.[15] Captain Steve Jaureguizar, the commander of the *Roosevelt*'s air wing, later recounted to investigators that Crozier told him simply: "This is going to end my career."[16]

Crozier was right. Someone leaked the email and the

letter to the *San Francisco Chronicle*, which verified its authenticity and published it on March 31. The documents embarrassed the Trump administration by demonstrating COVID-19's high virulence despite officials' downplaying of its seriousness. Although it was on the other side of the world, the plight of the *Roosevelt* mirrored the plight of the average American: feeling isolated by circumstance and confused by unreliable information. But Crozier and the *Roosevelt*'s leadership, to say nothing of the broader Navy, saw the leak as an unwelcome and embarrassing development. "Welp . . . there goes the neighborhood," one senior leader quipped.[17]

Two days later, on April 2, Acting Secretary of the Navy Modly removed Crozier from his command of the *Roosevelt*, citing his "extremely poor judgment" in sending the March 30 email and its leaking to the press. But the wheels kept turning: Modly himself resigned five days later after his infamous speech to the crew of the *Roosevelt* went viral on social media. To this day, fortunately, only one person on the *Roosevelt* died from complications of COVID-19: Chief Petty Officer Charles Robert Thacker Jr., who passed on April 13. The outbreak was not worse largely because the ship's population was young, strong, and healthy.

On April 29, the Navy planned to announce the findings of its initial investigation around the circumstances of the

March 30 email and its leak to the press. By many reports, the Navy was set to recommend Crozier's reinstatement as the commander of the *Roosevelt.* Instead, at the urging of the new acting secretary of the Navy, James McPherson (a retired judge advocate general and rear admiral), probably under pressure from the chairman of the Joint Chiefs and the secretary of defense, the investigation was widened to examine all the events leading up to the March 30 email. Outside political pressure, probably from the White House, seemed to be at play. At one press conference, the then president Trump mockingly said that Crozier should stop thinking of himself as "Hemingway," a slap at him writing the email.

This second investigation concluded on June 19 and the Navy reversed its initial position, denying Crozier's reinstatement to command of the *Roosevelt* and effectively freezing any future promotions for him. The about-face was based on Crozier's operational decisions during the outbreak. It cited the slow removal of infected sailors from the ship when first reaching Guam based on his preference to ensure the sailors' "comfort over safety" when the situation devolved.[18] It also cited the email's bypassing of members of Crozier's chain of command, namely his immediate superiors in Carrier Strike Group Nine and Seventh Fleet. Supporters of the relief-for-cause view say that Crozier cracked under the pressure, that the March 30 email was a desperate attempt to fix his previous mistakes, and that he subverted the chain of command with little forethought.[19] Detractors of the Navy's actions say that Crozier did what was necessary to break a bureaucratic logjam and that the Navy's decision to discipline him ended up being Monday-morning quarterbacking.[20]

What was on Crozier's mind as his finger hovered over the send button on March 30? It is important to remember the confined nature of an aircraft carrier. It is true that we in the Navy like to boast about the size of our carriers and the complexity of their operations. The *Roosevelt* is 1,092 feet long, roughly the size of the Empire State Building if laid on its side. It rises twenty stories off the water, is made of 47,000 tons of steel, when floated displaces 100,000 tons, and needs 5,700 people to operate it. As a former Fletcher School and Naval War College professor Dr. Toshi Yoshihara likes to say: "Operating a carrier is an act of national will."

But do not let the dimensions fool you: the carrier is a small place for the number of people on board. Most of the impressive real estate is taken up by the runway and storage for its aircraft. The places where the crew sleep make cheap New York apartments look like luxury accommodations. An individual sleeping bunk, called a "rack" in Navy slang, has the spaciousness of your average coffin. Places where food is prepared and served? Cramped. Work spaces? Cramped. Hallways? Cramped. Doorways are the size of a single mid-size individual. In other words: being on a Navy ship is one of the worst places to combat a virus like COVID-19. These tightly packed conditions weighed on Crozier as he evaluated his options.

A naval commander is responsible for the health and morale of the crew, and Crozier's sailors were getting desperate. Unlike in eras past, sailors' information was not just limited to official channels and crowdsourced rumors. These are twenty-first-century sailors, each armed with a cell phone with instant access to the unfolding global crisis. It was an information inverse of the carrier's cramped interiors. They were watching deaths rise, national borders close, and entire countries' populations go into lockdown. They relayed concerns from their "metal floating prison" to their loved ones back home, which then ended up filtering back to other members of Navy leadership and even to members of Congress.

Indeed, the mental state of the crew can be seen in the moving goodbye video for Captain Crozier. Amid the cheering and chanting for their departing captain, you will notice several things *not* happening: no social distancing, no masks. This happened not because the crew was reckless or ignorant of the virus's effects, as later interviewees in the investigation claim.[21] The crew knew exactly what was happening and just assumed that they all had the virus whether showing symptoms or not. The video shows the fatalism that infected the crew, a feeling Crozier understood when making the choices he did.

So how did Brett Crozier make the hard choice to send the email that he did?

First, he tried to gather as much science and fact as he could. Sadly, in those early days, not enough was known about the nature of the pathogen, its transmission paths, how to prevent much of the spread, the impact of mask wearing, and much more. He was forced to operate with incomplete information about a truly implacable but invisible foe. From what he knew, he was deeply concerned about the potential for a high mortality rate in his crew. Brett Crozier is a thoughtful, methodical planner who speaks in articulate and well-constructed paragraphs. He is a long way from an impulsive Halsey, and someone who thinks through his actions and comments.

But information was limited where Crozier needed it most. It is a truism in the national security community that you make decisions using the best available information at the time. Within his ship, Crozier was effectively flying blind: at the height of the crisis before the March 30 email,

Crozier and his staff estimated they had five hundred to six hundred cases, but they had no way of knowing for certain.[22] And with so little information about COVID-19 available at the time, extreme quarantine and deep-cleaning protocols seemed the only options for combating the spread. As it turned out, bleaching the ship's surfaces was only somewhat effective—and there were already twice as many cases aboard as Crozier and his senior staff had estimated.[23] And as we learned throughout the long course of the pandemic, the chances of contracting COVID from a surface are negligible. The key, we now know, is physical separation—something impossible to achieve on a carrier, no matter how often you scrub the handrails with bleach. Even as he tried to gather more facts, Crozier was also receiving extremely limited information from his chain of command, especially about the progress of negotiations for hotel rooms on Guam.[24]

A second complicated issue weighing on Crozier was the context of that precise moment in the six-month deployment of *Roosevelt*. The ship was not engaged in combat operations, nor was such a possibility looming on the horizon. Crozier has repeatedly said if it had been a combat situation, he would have continued to operate the ship "as normal" and accepted casualties from the virus. But he felt that given the ship was in a noncombat role at the time of the outbreak, he needed to put the health of his crew first, as I believe most commanders would do.

Third, Crozier had to decide on an accelerated schedule in real time. While not the equivalent of the minute-to-minute pressures of hot combat, the timeline he faced was very pressing to say the least. The Navy wanted the ship underway and back at sea to meet long-established commitments. He did not have the luxury of simply waiting for events to clarify. It is always good advice to take another full night's sleep, look at that email you drafted in the cold light of morning, before hitting send. But events closed in on Brett Crozier relentlessly.

He also suffered from confusion in his chain of command, a sort of "too many cooks spoiling the broth" syndrome. From the various levels in his chain, he often received conflicting guidance and changing sets of ideas. He became particularly frustrated with his three-star boss, the commander of Seventh Fleet, and fatefully left him off the addressee list on the red-flare email.

Fifth and finally, it is worth recalling that everything was happening in the glare of national and international publicity. Stories about the outbreak on the carrier were running at the top of the news hours on the 24-7 channels, the Navy was under visible pressure from a White House heading toward an election later in the year, and every move was being scrutinized.

Brett Crozier held a very bad hand of cards as he made his choice. He knew his "red flare" would risk it all in the context of his career—but he chose the health of his crew over anything else.

Learning from Crozier's hard choice must begin by acknowledging the fractious conversation it generated within the broader Navy. One of the main threads of the criticism is a perception that Crozier put the comfort of the crew ahead of the carrier's primary mission to protect the United States and its interests. Crozier's detractors see his actions either as a cowardly surrender to an evolving crisis or a heartfelt but misguided attempt to save lives at the expense of his primary responsibility in his role as commander. Military service of any kind carries an inherent risk to life and limb; that is part of the deal when you sign up. Indeed, the Navy has a history of daring individuals—like Jones, Decatur, and Farragut—who risked their crews in pursuit of their objectives, as we've discussed earlier in this volume.

But there is a key difference we must consider between those men and Crozier: the tactical objectives each pursued. Jones, Decatur, and Farragut all took great *calculated* risks in the heat of battle and in the context of hot wars. Crozier, on the other hand, was transiting between ports after a diplomatic visit in peacetime. If Farragut had put his crew's life in the same danger during a routine port call as he did when he charged Mobile Bay, he would not have been celebrated; he would have been fired. Crozier's situation is much closer to Pete Bucher's: boxed in by circumstances with the risk of losing human life over a very unclear objective.

It is also important to remember that so often the hard choice you make is something you have to live with from that moment forward. Had Crozier been so focused on his Navy career instead of the health of his crew, he likely would have continued to go along with the shifting guidance without raising any additional complications or hesitations. Had he done that, I suspect he would have never been fired by the acting secretary of the Navy, never been investigated for the events that led up to the outbreak, and likely would have continued with his Navy career and pinned on admiral's stars as I'd envisioned back in 2011.

An important point here is simple: communication is key. Communication breakdowns resulted in Crozier being unaware of the existing progress with Guam over the hotel rooms. New methods of communication allowed the crew to be informed of what was happening in the broader COVID crisis; many family members back in the United States followed the drama over social media. The pace of digital communications also made it difficult for all the players involved in solving the crisis to remain coordinated.

Many of the chain-of-command issues identified in the Navy's investigation could be boiled down to who was on what video conference, or which people were cc'd on emails. This only gets more complicated within the military's labyrinthian structure. At any given time, the *Roosevelt*'s COVID crisis was getting inputs from multiple levels of its own leadership, Carrier Strike Group Nine, Naval Base Guam, Joint Region Marianas, Seventh Fleet, Naval Air Forces Pacific, the Pacific Fleet commander, the commander of US Indo-Pacific Command, and the Pentagon. The idea of "fog of war" is nothing new, but the modern communications landscape requires a new set of skills for leaders to succeed.

Organizations also need to consider the culture of the people that they need to do a job. The Navy cannot expect to train individuals for decisive action and independent operation when necessary on the one hand and then express frustration when they take initiative after days of bureaucratic delays during a crisis. Members of the military need to accept orders from the chain of command, but that does not make them automatons who function only when told what to do. In the absence of direction, they will find a way to try to make things work. And if they take courageous actions like Brett Crozier, they end up doing their duty and dealing with the personal consequences later.

More than any other decision-maker in this book with the exception of Lloyd Bucher and John Paul Jones, Crozier was forced to play a very bad hand of cards. When I ask myself what I would have done differently, the short answer is not much. I, too, would have recognized the lack of information, the press of time, the glare of publicity, the poor job the Navy chain of command was doing, and that I was facing a clear career-ending moment. But I like to think I would have sent the red-flare email as well. Being a cautious sort of commander, I'm reasonably sure I would have sent it on a classified channel and included the commander of the numbered fleet. And I would, I hope, have had a more open relationship with my immediate superior, embarked in the carrier and living a few yards down the passageway. But those are essentially foot faults. My own assessment is that Crozier did the right thing sending the email, given the facts in hand and the context of the moment. He put concern for his crew—in a peacetime context—at the top of his priority list.

In the summer of 2020, as all this unfolded, many naval officers chimed in to criticize Brett Crozier. Among them was a smart nuclear submarine officer and close friend who had been a key part of my team at Deep Blue.* He laid out a cogent case criticizing Crozier, which he later published in a nationally syndicated newspaper. He sent me a copy to review, and I thanked him for it, but replied:

> I'd say neither of us have all the facts in hand, nor did we walk in Brett Crozier's shoes. I've heard from the highest levels of the uniformed service that he [Crozier] did in fact reach out along all the lines you mention and the system wasn't moving. I'd love to know the full timeline of what he tried first. You and I both know he didn't just launch this missile [the red-flare email] without trying a ton of other things, and I've heard exactly that from a variety of solid sources. I'm not much of an advocate for the Inspector General staff, but this one screams for a clear "tick tock" of what he tried first, what response he got, and what the Navy was doing. People don't commit career suicide lightly. So, point one is that there is a lack of real facts to judge here.
>
> Rarely do you and I part company in views, and I am all for the chain of command; but on this one I think there are definitely two sides to the story. I agree that

---

* Deep Blue was a small, nimble think tank created immediately after 9/11 that I led as a one-star rear admiral. It had a handpicked group of officers charged with coming up with ideas for the Navy to employ in the emerging Global War on Terror.

Crozier should not have sent an UNCLS [unclassified] email to a couple of dozen Flags (he did not send it to any civilian, by the way), and he DID include his chain of command, but added some other Flags. But clearly he did so because the Navy was not taking him seriously and he did what he felt he needed to for his crew.

Note that he was relieved not by any uniformed Flag in his chain, but by the SECNAV. I've never seen that, it tells you where the active duty Flag chain of command is on this one. A better course for the Navy would have been to let him handle the offloading/sanitization of the ship, and his strike group commander could have appropriately indicated dissatisfaction in a FITREP [fitness report] downrange. But firing and publicly humiliating him is overkill, and hurts him, of course, but hurts the Navy as well. It sends a bad signal to other Commanding Officers. I think it was a mistake on the part of the Navy, on balance.

Subsequent to that exchange, after a preliminary investigation, the chief of naval operations went forward with a recommendation to reinstate Crozier in command. That was overruled by the chairman of the Joint Chiefs and the secretary of defense, who directed that the Navy conduct further review. When that second, more detailed investigation was completed, the chain of command upheld Brett's relief for cause.

In my view, the Navy had it right by recommending his reinstatement, and I believe some level of political pressure was exerted from the White House. Brett Crozier's career was ended, and he will retire in the summer of 2022 as a captain without further disciplinary action. He made captain in the Navy and commanded a nuclear aircraft carrier and led his squadron of jet fighters in combat—a fine record. I know him well personally, and I predict he will make a strong transition to the civilian world, where I hope he will use his leadership and decision-making skills to inform others. I'd gladly have him on my team again, and I will always be thankful for his fine work during the Libyan campaign and for his overall service to the nation.

I believe this case study will be examined by generations of naval officers going forward, and with good reason. It perfectly outlines for the Navy the principles of caring for the crew and the difficulty of balancing that with getting the mission done. People versus mission is an age-old dilemma for sea captains. There are no easy answers, and the need to find that balance between deep concern for the team as a "servant leader" and the external demands to get the job done exist in business, medicine, education, family life, and really throughout society. The ultimate lesson of Brett

Crozier is that the choices will be hard, your actions will unlikely be perfect, there will be lots of criticism from those who weren't there, but you make your best choice and hold your head high, come what may. Captain Brett Crozier certainly can hold his head up proudly and should sail on with pride.

Conclusion

The most difficult thing is the decision to act, the
rest is merely tenacity. The fears are paper tigers.
You can do anything you decide to do. You can act
to change and control your life; and the procedure,
the process is its own reward.

AMELIA EARHART

In any moment of decision, the best thing you
can do is the right thing, the next best thing is
the wrong thing, and the worst thing you can
do is nothing.

THEODORE ROOSEVELT

When I was a young teenager, I remember marveling at my father's approach to making a hard decision. He would get out a yellow legal pad and draw a line vertically down the center of the page. Then he would put a big + sign on one side, and a – sign on the other. Finally, he'd spend considerable time putting down all the pros and cons of a particular course of action under the + and – signs. I saw him use the technique multiple times, but perhaps most meaningfully as he wrestled with the decision whether or not to retire from the US Marine Corps in 1970. At that time, he was a full colonel with a chest full of medals from the Korean War and had recently returned from a highly successful thirteen-month combat tour in Vietnam during which he commanded a reinforced Marine battalion around Da Nang. The Corps was offering him a plum assignment in Newport, Rhode Island, at the US Naval War College.

He would be eligible for consideration for promotion to one-star brigadier general within a year or two. All of that went down on the pro side of staying in. On the con side went down things like future family separation with an almost certain additional combat tour in Vietnam (a war that didn't look like it was going to end anytime soon at that point in the late 1960s). In addition to separation, he listed uncertainty about promotion prospects (a tiny percentage of Marine colonels ever get that coveted step to one-star) and the need to move at least a couple of times over the next few years (disrupting high school timing for me and my sister). He also added pros and cons about his age and timing to shift to a new career, availability of scholarships for a PhD program in education (his aspiration after the Marines was to become a senior administrator and eventually a president at a college or university), our family financial situation, and a host of other things.

Once he had his lists down, he spoke with my mom, and then with me and my sister, and with mentors on both the USMC side and in the civilian world. He then mentally totaled it all up and made his decision: he retired as a full colonel, began drawing his retirement pension, got a scholarship in a PhD program at Arizona State University, and off we went to Tempe, Arizona. It was a textbook example of how to make a big life decision in a sensible, rational, and unemotional way. While initially I wasn't thrilled about moving to the desert of the Southwest, I made the best of it for my final two years of high school and retain good memories of those years before I went off to Annapolis and a career in the US Navy. Part of how I was able to deal with that kind of turbulence was that I had great faith in my father's decision-making. And it worked out well for him. After earning a PhD in the administration of higher education, he landed a dream job at Community College of Allegheny County (one of the largest in the United States) in the Pittsburgh area, eventually serving as president before retiring to Florida in the early 1980s.

His methodical style of decision-making has a lot to commend it, but as we have learned in the course of writing this book, there isn't always time, resources, or even the right personality to get out a legal pad and start jotting down the pros and cons. It's hard to imagine John Paul Jones scribbling a few notes on yellow paper (even the color is wrong), or Dorie Miller weighing the pros and cons of rushing quite literally to the sound of the guns. For some of the other figures in this book, there would have been more time. Michelle Howard or Brett Crozier might have had the luxury of a bit more time, but even there we see decision-makers reacting to circumstances under considerable pressure of time and with outside observers—not all benign—leaning in at every second. So, recognizing that many choices are made under pressure, with limited time for reflection, what are some of the keys to making fast, sensible, ethical, and ultimately successful decisions? What can we learn from the nine hard choices we have studied?

First, it is important to remember that organizations are always shaped by important choices. The very ethos of the US Navy changed over time, very much influenced by the impact of these hard choices on the broader service. My thesis, as I conclude this work, is that decision-makers in any endeavor can learn from these experiences about how to make the hard choices life presents us.

Above all, decision-makers can gather intelligence, process information, weigh alternatives, connect "ends, ways, and means," and make their choices. The "furious pressure of combat" is unique, but it does offer lessons. Decision-makers can and must function differently under pressure— even short of combat—than they do in more measured times, and they can most certainly learn about how we make choices in our own lives from these stories. Another way to think of this is that the Navy is in many ways a reflection of the country. In addition to what we learn about the Navy and its evolution from these nine decisions, these choices also reflect the nation's sense of accountability, risk, and honor more broadly. They also make for a pretty good collection of ways to approach decision-making, especially when we consciously list them and over time get into the habit of using them—even in tense, fast-moving situations. So, what are the tools and approaches that can help those making decisions? Let's look at the key elements.

Gather all the intelligence. So often our choices are made with a faulty understanding of the simple facts of the case. In particular, we should be aware of the phenomenon of "belief bias," which is applying what you think ought to be happening to what is actually unfolding. The classic case of this in the Navy world was the shoot-down of an Iranian commercial aircraft by USS *Vincennes*, a brand-new AEGIS cruiser in the Arabian Gulf in July 1988. In the stories in this volume, several of the naval officers chose to very aggressively seek intelligence, notably Admiral Farragut before sailing into Mobile Bay and Admiral Dewey prior to engaging the Spanish fleet at Manila Bay. In particular, beware of confusing assumptions (things you think are true) and facts (things that are indisputably true). With the departure of the Trump administration in 2021, we have hopefully heard the last of "alternative facts," a phrase made infamous by Kellyanne Conway. Knowing what is real and what is not is crucial; gathering intelligence relentlessly before moving to decision-making is also crucial.

Understand the timeline. Very often people approaching decisions put themselves under artificial or self-imposed deadlines. Pushing back to get more time before committing is always worth attempting. You should never commit to a course of action before you must. A good example of this from the cases before us was the way in which Admiral Dewey deliberately marshaled all the logistics at his disposal, waited for the human intelligence to arrive in the form of reports from a US diplomat from the Philippines, and dragged out his timeline as far as he possibly could. Again and again, I've seen various bosses I've worked for avoid "lunging at the ball," instead finding a bit more time and space to make an informed decision. The best of all in this regard was Secretary of the Navy Richard Danzig, who could at times be a bit maddening in how he would ask for more information, another report from the fleet, a re-briefing on options. But over more than two years as his executive assistant and senior Navy aide, I never saw him make a bad decision, from pushing for women to be assigned to nuclear submarines to investigating a terrible collateral-damage bombing incident on the island of Vieques in the Caribbean. President Barack Obama, for whom I served for over four years as Supreme Allied Commander at NATO, also had that kind of patient, "wait for the facts" attitude, and refused to be budged on a decision until he was comfortable he had all the facts, or events simply demanded the choice be made.

Methodically consider the possible outcomes of your decision—both good and bad. This sounds so obvious, but on countless occasions I've seen smart, gifted people make a decision without really considering the full range of outcomes, especially in the negative direction. In the extraordinary science fiction novel *Dune* by Frank Herbert, the protagonist uses a drug that allows him to simultaneously see the entire web of events that occurs down each leg of the timeline that could flow from his decisions. Perhaps fortunately, we are not possessed of the ability to simply mentally walk ourselves down the "consequence lines" of our choices, evaluate how each comes out, *then* come back to the present and make the decision.

What we *can* do as normal humans is consciously and deliberately think through the major potential outcomes of a given decision and evaluate their impact on what we are trying to accomplish. When she was contemplating the hostage-rescue operation for Captain Phillips, the then rear admiral Michelle Howard had to look at the range of potential outcomes—a clean success including the capture of the pirates; a failure and the death of Captain Phillips; some mixture of the two, with Phillips receiving a severe or a lesser wound, perhaps accidentally shot by a SEAL; the pirates negotiating a conclusion; and on and on. In this phase of decision-making, it is important to neither take counsel excessively of your fears *nor* become emotionally involved in an unrealistic result. Good decision-makers can boil the outcomes down to three or four or five realistic scenarios, then evaluate them against one another. The key is being brutally honest about the range of outcomes.

Evaluate the resources. This requires clear-eyed skepticism. Necessary supplies will almost never arrive early, equipment will break down, events will tend to stretch out, people will get tired, and so forth. In the disastrous Iranian hostage-rescue effort in 1979 known as Desert One, pretty much everything that could go wrong did go wrong. The decision-makers should have anticipated the failure rates and programmed more buffer into the system. Those lessons were deeply absorbed by the special operations community, which has evolved into the most planning-oriented part of the US military. As I was anticipating the chances of a hostage-rescue operation in Colombia in 2006–09, I was astounded by the level of detail and redundancy built into the work of the special operations teams from the Delta Force assigned to work with me. They had an enormous level of resources available, including an exact mock-up of the jungle clearing where we thought the hostages were being held, which was used to rehearse endlessly. This had a positive effect on my thinking as a decision-maker.

On the other hand, consider the paucity of resources that Pete Bucher had in USS *Pueblo*: a green crew, a few small arms, a frozen crew-served weapon on deck, and no air cover. As he worked hard to think his way through a truly terrible scenario, he had to quickly calculate the resources available. Had he known that there was a possibility of air cover arriving, his calculus might have been different. A key element in any decision is what you have to draw upon as you move to execution.

Focus on your people—but don't be paralyzed with fear over their well-being. Whether you are leading a five-thousand-person crew on an aircraft carrier like Captain Brett Crozier, or a three-person team on the sales force at Google, as a decision-maker you have an obligation to understand the impact your choices will have on the people working for you. That does not mean you should become paralyzed with the thought that some of your people will suffer, especially in a military context. Finding the balance between literally "throwing people at the problem" (like many US Civil War commanders, or generals in WWI on both sides of the fighting lines did) and taking calculated risks while keeping the mission and objective firmly in sight is the key. In this book, the scale runs from a John Paul Jones, who was utterly willing to risk the lives and limbs of his men, to a Brett Crozier, who sacrificed his career to put his crew's health at the top of his priority list.

As a general proposition, in both the military and the civilian world, we have become more predisposed to value the lives and well-being of our teams in recent decades—a good thing. The idea of servant leadership is infused with a deep concern about the people on the team. But there will come a time—both in military operations and civilian contexts—where leaders must put the mission ahead of the people.

Don't get emotionally involved in people who are roadblocks. One of the greatest books ever written about leadership and decision-making is Mario Puzo's twentieth-century classic *The Godfather.* In one memorable scene early in the novel, Don Corleone is approached by an ambitious hoodlum who wants to use the Don's networks and connections to facilitate a business in drugs. The Don is not willing to let him do so and patiently explains his rationale to the ambitious hood. Don Corleone's impulsive son Santino blurts out a question that might imply support for the proposition, and the Don rebukes him publicly. Later, after an assassination attempt on the Don fails, Santino leads the family "to the mattresses" and to war. He becomes deeply and emotionally involved with avenging his father and makes several mistakes, including one that leads to his own death. His far more cold-blooded brother Michael takes over and goes on to demonstrate his ability to make emotion-free decisions required for the good of the family, following the traditions of Don Corleone. The book and the films are replete with examples of decision-making both good and bad, and a central lesson is never to hate your enemies, because it can cloud your judgment—and your decision-making skills.

Be willing to change your mind. I remember when I first took the venerable college entrance exam, then called the Scholastic Aptitude Test (SAT), the advice I received was "go with your first answer." I followed the advice, even when I read over the question again and thought, "Wait a minute, I bet that isn't right." Over time, studies have shown that the idea of always going with the first answer that occurs to you actually creates a *lower* probability of a correct answer. Decision-makers should be willing to assess a situation and change their mind, very often improving the outcome they seek.

In his excellent book *Think Again*, Adam Grant explores in depth the idea of changing your mind and going against conventional thinking, and he relates a particularly poignant example. Basing his storytelling on Norman Maclean's extraordinary book *Young Men and Fire*, he tells the tale of the

Mann Gulch, Montana, fire in 1949, in which the majority of a team of fifteen young, fit, highly trained fire jumpers (firefighters who parachute into a forest fire to fight it) were killed trying to outrace a fire across a dry meadow. They literally tried to outrun the fire, but because of their training, most of them refused to drop their heavy gear. One of the few survivors was the team foreman who, obviously acting under intense pressure, dropped to the ground and "burned out" a mini firebreak around himself, covered up with a blanket, and was able to survive—because the fire had no fuel in his immediate vicinity to burn. He literally went against what he'd been trained to do and did so in the most dangerous moment.[1] Being prepared to step out of line with previous training can sometimes be the best decision of all.

Be determined. So often, decision-making is hard because we dither, worrying about what will occur. You can never predict the future with complete certainty, of course, but determination—a willful approach to problems—can be a tonic in such moments of indecision. When I find myself mentally shuttling back and forth between options, I try to think about John Paul Jones. He was wrong in many things in his very eventful life, but the reason he is remembered today is that he was ruthlessly determined about a key decision he made in USS *Bonhomme Richard*—to fight on.

Be prepared to execute. Decision-making is actually not

the end of most situations, but often the beginning. Even as you mentally conclude with the choice ahead of you, realize that communicating and advocating the decision is often as important as generating it—understanding what just happened in the process of making the choice, rapidly developing the plan to execute it, applying the resources that you've evaluated, and beginning the operations are, of course, all crucial to how the decision will look in time. The execution of the decision is crucial. Finding balance by not allowing 'the desire for perfect to become the enemy of good enough' is fundamental to the art of decision. We need to understand that measuring the *outcome* of a given choice—monitoring and metrics—is vital. Declaring success, knowing how to telegraph success, the use of optimism as a force multiplier in decision-making, and knowing when to "find the exit" are all key themes that echo through these choices.

All decisions have consequences, and with hard choices come high risks—but potentially deeply satisfying outcomes. Perspective and balance are crucial in evaluating the choices we make—and in getting the hardest decisions to come out right. We've spent time looking at nine hard decisions in the course of this book, and each of them is a true story, told with as much accuracy and empathy as I can muster. But I'd like to conclude with a pair of fictional naval decision-makers to illustrate the point that there is so much to learn about decision-making from stories (especially when they are based on real events). Coincidentally, both stories involved destroyers operating in the icy waters of the North Atlantic, although one is about a very bad decision and the other an exemplar of good decision-making.

The first is that old Cold War classic *The Bedford Incident*, the novel by Mark Rascovich. Set in the waters of the so-called Greenland-Iceland-United Kingdom "gap," it is the story of a pitched battle between an elite American destroyer—the USS *Bedford* of the title—and a Russian nuclear submarine. The American destroyer captain is a "hot runner" in Navy parlance, destined for an admiral's stars, and he becomes obsessed with finding and forcing the Soviet submarine to the surface with very aggressive anti-submarine warfare techniques including a powerful sonar. As the novel unfolds, he comes closer and closer to his prey—much like Ahab chasing Moby Dick—and is holding the boat down and tracking it closely. As he converses with a subordinate who questions the aggressive behavior, he says, "If he fires one [a torpedo], I'll fire one." A young officer manning the firing console nearby misunderstands the comment and interprets it as a command to fire at the submarine, which he does. The submarine is destroyed, and the potential implications—a hot war between the United States and Soviet Union—become clear. To forestall such a war, an embarked Ger-

man officer—ironically a World War II U-boat veteran—
deliberately destroys the American destroyer to "even the
score" and avoid a war. The American destroyer captain's decision to obsessively pursue the Soviet submarine, arm his
weapons, and hang on the edge of an attack caused a fatal
mistake that lost him his ship, his crew, and his own life. He
became emotionally involved with his prey, didn't fully think
through negative outcomes, and disregarded the well-being
of his crew (and himself), all while misunderstanding the
level of resources and control he held. It was a tragic decision,
and the consequences are powerfully outlined in the novel.
The black-and-white 1965 film, with Richard Widmark playing the commanding officer, is also a classic, and the "If he
fires one, I'll fire one" scenario is often used in military training classes to this day.

The other novel that is a portrait of a series of good decisions at sea made in real-world stress is by C. S. Forester: *The
Good Shepherd*. Recently made into a noteworthy film star-
ring Tom Hanks called *Greyhound*, the book follows the exploits of a convoy commander (played by Hanks) who spends
several sleepless nights on the bridge of his destroyer. The
convoy is attacked by a pack of U-boats, called a "wolf pack,"
and one by one the ships under his protection are picked off.
Yet he consistently makes smart tactical decisions, leading
to destroying several of the U-boats and eventually making

his way to the British side of the North Atlantic with "only" the loss of a handful of commercial ships and one of the four destroyers under his command. In both the book and the film, we see a commander (the "Good Shepherd" of the title) using the tools described above—carefully absorbing intelligence; prolonging the time he has to make individual decisions when he can by maneuvering the convoy; avoiding becoming emotionally involved, particularly after being taunted over the bridge-to-bridge radio by U-boat commanders; husbanding his resources; thinking through outcomes, both good and bad; and applying true grit and determination to a grim scenario. While he loses some of his ships, his tactical decisions are grounded in the overall strategic objective of getting the majority of the ships through, which is achieved. The book and the film are in effect a master class in decision-making in the crucible of extreme stress.

And so, we come to the end of this voyage through the process of decision-making. In both of the cases above, on the bridge of a destroyer, a captain decides "to risk it all." I, too, have stood on a destroyer's bridge as the captain and faced difficult choices a fair number of times, although none as hard as either of the captains above. But I know the pressure of such moments, when time seems to compress, and options become more limited with every tick of the clock. That is the moment when I have tried to make time slow down, at least in my own frame of mind. It is when your voice should become calmer, your breathing more regular, your information scanning more deliberate—all of which is easy to say and very, very hard to do. Some of the "tricks of the trade" are outlined above, but let me end with a final thought: the ability to make good decisions is like a muscle—it must be exercised carefully, trained to perform at peak readiness, and treated with respect.

We all make dozens of decisions every day, but once in a great while some of us must make truly hard decisions under a high degree of pressure, often with little time to ponder the pros and cons. A significant part of making the best possible decision under those circumstances involves what we do in the years before we face it. Thus, that conscious preparation, lifelong study, and the cultivation of a willingness to act and avoid paralysis in the face of crisis become the keys to facing a crisis—knowing all the while that what we decide may well not result in the outcomes we want.

Indeed, we all must face the simple fact that no one's decisions are always right—I have made bad choices too many times to count. But whenever I've been faced with a truly hard choice, both at sea and ashore, I've put my faith in what I've learned along the voyage of life, at first from my parents and teachers, over time from my family and friends, and to some degree from the hard preparation of studying history and looking for role models who sailed before me. My sincerest wish with *To Risk It All* is that you never in fact have to risk it all. But if you do, my hope is that by reading this book and contemplating these sailors, you will have gained a better chance of making the right choice and thus finding the elusive balance between impulsive determination and thoughtful consideration—in the very crucible of decision.

Godspeed and open water in all the choices you make.

ACKNOWLEDGMENTS

My earliest and best teachers in the world of making choices were my parents, George and Shirley. We were a close family and lived all over the world due to my father's career as an officer in the US Marine Corps. Wherever we went, I saw my parents making the right choices for our family. And I watched as a very young teenager as my father chose to go to Vietnam and into combat to serve our nation, a decision that helped me ultimately choose to follow him into military service.

Along the years of my early education, I was lucky to encounter brilliant teachers, especially at the US Naval Academy from 1972 to 1976. In many conversations and courses studying maritime history, sea literature, leadership, and ethics at Annapolis, I explored examples of those who have faced the hardest of choices. Much of my foundational thinking about the idea of making decisions in high-stress environments began there in the novels of Herman Wouk, the plays of William Shakespeare, and the classic histories of E. B. Potter—one of my most distinguished professors.

In the course of my long career in the Navy, I had the privilege of serving for both officers and civilian leaders who were forced to make very hard decisions in peace and war. Among the leaders who have helped and mentored me whom I most associate with the ability to make difficult choices at speed in the crucible of extreme pressure are Admiral Carl Trost, General Colin Powell, Admiral Vern Clark, Admiral Fox Fallon, Admiral Harry Harris, Admiral Bob Natter, General Jim Mattis, and Vice Admiral Cutler Dawson. Civilian leaders include Sean O'Keefe, Richard Danzig, Don Rumsfeld, Leon Panetta, and Chuck Hagel. In particular, working for Secretary of Defense Bob Gates sharpened my own ability to make tough choices. None of the leaders I have mentioned were perfect decision-makers—no one ever is, of course—but I learned from each of them and some of their ideas have made their way into this book.

The initial idea for this book was suggested by my shipmate and dear friend Captain Bill Harlow, and as always his editorial assistance and clear-eyed advice have been crucial to its creation—he is the ultimate true professional. As a concept it benefited immensely from the thoughts of my superb and patient editor, Scott Moyers of Penguin Press. Many thanks to Scott's entire team, especially Liz Calamari and Mia Council. Likewise, I am deeply grateful to my literary agent, Andrew Wylie, who continues to help guide my career as a writer in this, my twelfth book. My two research assistants, Matt Merighi and Colin Steele, both of whom were stellar graduate students at the Fletcher School of Law and Diplomacy during my deanship, were instrumental in creating the individual narrative histories of the characters in this volume. As the book matured, it benefited from fact-checking by the team at the Naval History and Heritage Command, led by my friend Rear Admiral Sam Cox, USN (Ret.).

Finally, my wife, Laura, as usual was gracious and understanding on the many weekends when I took time away from her (and her beloved pickleball court) to read again the many books of history, leadership, and ethics that helped me shape the arc of this narrative. Along with our two daughters, Christina and Julia, Laura is the North Star of my life. Falling in love with her was the easiest and best choice I've ever made.

To all of these and many others too numerous to mention, I send my deepest thanks. As always, their efforts are the best of this volume, and the errors and misjudgments are mine alone.

NOTES

EPIGRAPH

1. John Fitzgerald Kennedy, quoted in *Essence of Decision: Explaining the Cuban Missile Crisis* by Graham Allison (Boston: Little Brown, 1971).

INTRODUCTION

1. Azi Paybarah, "The USS Johnston Sank in 1944: A Crew Just Visited Its Wreckage," *The New York Times*, April 9, 2021, www.nytimes.com /2021/04/09/us/uss-johnston-navy-philippines.html.
2. Notably *Sea of Thunder* by Evan Thomas and *The Last Stand of the Tin Can Sailors* by James Hornfischer.

CHAPTER ONE: THE POWER OF "NO"

1. James Stavridis, *Sailing True North: Ten Admirals and the Voyage of Character* (New York: Penguin Press, 2019).
2. Evan Thomas, *John Paul Jones: Sailor, Hero, Father of the American Navy* (New York: Simon & Schuster, 2003), 8.
3. Thomas, 231.
4. Samuel Eliot Morison, *John Paul Jones: A Sailor's Biography* (Annapolis, MD: Naval Institute Press, 1989), 39–45.
5. Fletcher Pratt, *The Navy: A History* (New York: Garden City, 1941), 4–5.
6. James Fenimore Cooper, *The History of the Navy of the United States of America* (Annapolis, MD: Naval Institute Press, [1856] 2001), 77–78.
7. Thomas, *John Paul Jones*, 191.
8. Thomas, 192.
9. Winston Churchill, October 29, 1941, speech to Harrow School, https:// www.nationalchurchillmuseum.org/never-give-in-never-never-never .html.

CHAPTER TWO: A YOUNG MAN'S GAME

1. A. E. Hotchner, *Papa Hemingway: A Personal Memoir* (New York: Random House, 1966), 56.
2. See Ian Toll's brilliant book *Six Frigates*, which tells their story so well.
3. US Navy, "Statement of the circumstances attending the destruction of the frigate *Philadelphia*, with the names of the officers and the number of men employed on the occasion, as laid before the President by the Secretary of the Navy, November 13, 1804" in *Documents, Official and Unofficial, Relating to the Case of the Capture and Destruction of the Frigate Philadelphia, at Tripoli, on the 16th February 1804* (Washington, DC: John T. Towers, 1850), Naval History and Heritage Command, www.history.navy.mil/content/history/nhhc/research/library/online-reading-room/title-list-alphabetically/d/capture-and-destruction-of-the-frigate-philadelphia-at-tripoli-1850.html#SOF.
4. Benjamin Stoddert to John Adams, April 19, 1799, in United States, Office of Naval Records and Library, *Naval Documents Related to the Quasi-War between the United States and France*, vol. 3, *Naval Operations from April to July 1799* (Washington, DC: US Government Printing Office, 1936).
5. Robert J. Allison, *Stephen Decatur: American Naval Hero, 1779–1820* (Amherst: University of Massachusetts Press, 2005), 183–84. Like many historical sayings—such as "damn the torpedoes"—this is better known today in paraphrased form, but Decatur's sentiment is clear in the original.

CHAPTER THREE: RISKY BUSINESS

1. This is how the order was recorded by Farragut's son Loyall in his 1879 biography of his father, *The Life of David Glasgow Farragut, First Admiral of the United States Navy: Embodying His Journal and Letters* (New York: Appleton, 1879).
2. Brian Burrell, *Damn the Torpedoes: Fighting Words, Rallying Cries, and the Hidden History of Warfare* (New York: McGraw-Hill, 1999), 193.
3. "Detailed Report of Rear-Admiral Farragut, U.S. Navy, with Enclosures, August 12, 1864," Naval History and Heritage Command, www.history.navy.mil/research/library/online-reading-room/title-list-alphabetically/b/battle-of-mobile-bay.html.
4. "Detailed Report."
5. "Detailed Report."
6. "Detailed Report."
7. Donald Rumsfeld, *Known and Unknown: A Memoir* (New York: Penguin Press, 2011).

CHAPTER FOUR: COOL HAND GEORGE

1. Portions of this chapter were drawn from the author's *The Sailor's Bookshelf: Fifty Books to Know the Sea* (Annapolis, MD: Naval Institute Press, 2021).
2. Ronald Spector, *Admiral of the New Empire: The Life and Career of George Dewey* (New York: Viking, 2001).
3. George Dewey, *Autobiography of George Dewey* (Annapolis, MD: Naval Institute Press, 1987), 132.
4. Dewey, 61–95.
5. Eric Smith, introduction to *Autobiography of George Dewey* (Annapolis, MD: Naval Institute Press, 1987), xi.
6. Dewey, 5.
7. Edward S. Ellis, *Dewey and Other Naval Commanders* (New York: Hurst & Company, 1899), 7.
8. William Lawrence, *A Concise Life of Admiral George Dewey, U.S.N.* (Boston: J. F. Murphy, 1899), 35.
9. Dewey, *Autobiography*, 174–75.
10. Dewey, 196.
11. Dewey, 210.

CHAPTER FIVE: THE PROTECTOR

1. Doris Miller's Navy Cross Award citation. https://www.history.navy.mil/content/history/nhhc/browse-by-topic/diversity/african-americans/miller/doris-millers-navy-cross-citation.html#:~:text=CITATION%3A%20%22For%20distinguished%20devotion%20to,forces%20on%20December%207%2C%201941.
2. Thomas W. Cutrer and T. Michael Parrish, *Doris Miller, Pearl Harbor, and the Birth of the Civil Rights Movement* (College Station: Texas A&M University Press, 2018), chap. 2.
3. Cutrer and Parrish, chap. 1.
4. Cutrer and Parrish, chap. 3.
5. Rawn James, *The Double V: How Wars, Protest, and Harry Truman Desegregated America's Military* (New York: Bloomsbury, 2014), 129–30.
6. James, 131.
7. Doris Kearns Goodwin, *No Ordinary Time* (New York: Simon & Schuster, 2008).

CHAPTER SIX: THE WORLD WONDERS

1. Thomas Alexander Hughes, *Admiral Bill Halsey: A Naval Life* (Cambridge, MA: Harvard University Press, 2016), 48–49.
2. Evan Thomas, *Sea of Thunder: Four Commanders and the Last Great Naval Campaign, 1941–1945* (New York: Simon & Schuster, 2006), 220–22.
3. Thomas, 354.
4. E. B. Potter, *Bull Halsey* (Annapolis, MD: Naval Institute Press, 985), 303.

5. Hughes, *Admiral Bill Halsey*, 121.
6. Ronald H. Spector, *Eagle Against the Sun: The American War with Japan* (New York: Vintage, 1985), 18.
7. Thomas Buell, *The Quiet Warrior: A Biography of Admiral Raymond A. Spruance* (Boston: Little, Brown, 1974).
8. Walter Borneman, *The Admirals: Nimitz, Halsey, Leahy, and King—the Five-Star Admirals Who Won the War at Sea* (New York: Little, Brown, 2012), 157.
9. Potter, *Halsey*, 36–38.
10. Potter, 51.
11. Potter, 64.
12. Potter, 221.
13. Ian W. Toll, *Twilight of the Gods: War in the Western Pacific, 1944–1945* (New York: Norton, 2020), 114.
14. Halsey, quoted in Spector, *Eagle Against the Sun*, 431.
15. Spector, *Eagle Against the Sun*, 431–33.
16. Spector, 437–52.
17. Quoted in Spector, 438.
18. Toll, *Twilight of the Gods*, 278.
19. Commodore Arleigh Burke, Admiral Mitscher's chief of staff, quoted in Spector, *Eagle Against the Sun*, 433.

CHAPTER SEVEN: NO WAY OUT

1. Lloyd M. Bucher and Mark Rascovich, *Bucher: My Story* (Garden City, NY: Doubleday, 1970), 407.
2. H. W. Crocker III, *Don't Tread on Me* (New York: Crown Forum, 2006), 98.
3. Bucher and Rascovich, *Bucher*, 59
4. Bucher and Rascoviceh, *Bucher*, 8.
5. Mitchell B. Lerner, *The* Pueblo *Incident: A Spy Ship and the Failure of American Foreign Policy* (University Press of Kansas, 2002), 12.
6. Bucher and Rascovich, *Bucher*, 18.
7. Jack Cheevers, *Act of War: Lyndon Johnson, North Korea, and the Capture of the Spy Ship* Pueblo (New York: NAL Caliber, 2013), 9.

CHAPTER EIGHT: PIRATES OF THE GULF OF ADEN

1. Quoted in David Lerman, "Black Woman Named to a Top U.S. Navy Job Says Wimps Fail," *Bloomberg*, December 20, 2013, https://web.archive.org/web/20131229181819/http://www.bloomberg.com/news/print/2013-12-20/black-woman-named-to-a-top-u-s-navy-job-says-wimps-fail.html.
2. Marc Gonsalves, Keith Stansell, and Tom Howes, with Gary Brozek, *Out of Captivity: Surviving 1,967 Days in the Colombian Jungle* (New York: William Morrow, 2009).

3. "Operacion Militar Jaque . . . Orgullo por siempre," *Revista Ejército*, July 2009, no. 144.
4. Gonsalves et al., *Out of Captivity*, 439.
5. For more of this story, see the chapter on Admiral Zumwalt in James Stavridis, *Sailing True North: Ten Admirals and the Voyage of Character* (New York: Penguin Press, 2019).
6. Quoted in Lerman, "Black Woman Named to a Top U.S. Navy Job."
7. Quoted in Scott Wyland, "U.S. Navy's 1st Female 4-Star Admiral Set to Retire," *Stars and Stripes*, September 26, 2017, www.stripes.com /news/us-navy-s-1st-female-4-star-admiral-set-to-retire-1.489556.
8. For the timeline of events aboard the *Maersk Alabama* throughout the crisis, see Richard Phillips, *A Captain's Duty* (New York: Hyperion, 2010), and "Don't Give Up the Ship! Quick Thinking and a Boatload of Know-How Saves the MAERSK ALABAMA," *Marine Officer*, 2009, https://web.archive.org/web/20101103192007/http://mebaunion.org /WHATS-NEW/The_Real_Story_of_the_MAERSK_ALABAMA.pdf.
9. Quoted in Brock Vergakis, "She Helped Save Capt. Phillips from Somali Pirates. Then Became the First Female 4-Star Admiral," *The Virginian-Pilot*, February 28, 2020, www.pilotonline.com/military /vp-nw-hampton-roads-black-history-michelle-howard-navy-piracy -20200226-anjlah4tmbhxnbuviwdkdh3uri-story.html.

CHAPTER NINE: THE RED FLARE

1. Captain Brett Crozier email to his Navy superiors. https://www .military.com/daily-news/2020/03/31/sailors-do-not-need-die-carrier -captain-pleads-help-virus-cases-surge.html.
2. James Stavridis, *The Accidental Admiral: A Sailor Takes Command at NATO* (Annapolis, MD: Naval Institute Press, 2013).
3. Matthias Gafni and Joe Garofoli, "A Captain's Choice," *San Francisco Chronicle*.
4. Matthias Gafni and Joe Garofoli, "Exclusive: Captain of Aircraft Carrier with Growing Coronavirus Outbreak Pleads for Help from Navy," *San Francisco Chronicle*, March 31, 2020, www.sfchronicle.com /bayarea/article/Exclusive-Captain-of-aircraft-carrier-with-151 67883.php.
5. US Navy, "FOIA Request DON-NAVY-2020-00648, Parts 201–209," requested by Paul Szoldra on April 3, 2020, part 206, 20, www .muckrock.com/foi/united-states-of-america-10/emails-from-capt -brett-crozier-91301/#comms.
6. "Timeline: Theodore Roosevelt COVID-19 Outbreak Investigation," US Naval Institute News, June 23, 2020, https://news.usni.org/2020 /06/23/timeline-theodore-roosevelt-covid-19-outbreak-investigation.
7. US Navy, "Witness Statement of CAPT Brett Crozier USN," given May 8, 2020, 15, https://assets.documentcloud.org/documents/7212572/USS -Theodore-Roosevelt-Coronavirus-Crozier.pdf.

8. US Navy, "Witness Statement of CAPT Brett Crozier USN," 17.

9. Gina Harkins, "6 Big Takeaways from the Full Navy Investigation into a Carrier's COVID Outbreak," Military.com, September 19, 2020, www.military.com/daily-news/2020/09/19/6-big-takeaways-full -navy-investigation-carriers-covid-outbreak.html.

10. US Navy, "Witness Statement of CAPT Brett Crozier USN," 17.

11. Chief of Naval Operations, *Command Investigation Concerning Chain of Command Actions with Regard to COVID-19 Onboard USS Theodore Roosevelt (CVN-71)* (Washington, DC: US Navy, June 19, 2020), 317, https:// assets.documentcloud.org/documents/7212256/TR -Command-Investigation-with-Appendices.pdf.

12. US Navy, "Witness Statement of CAPT Brett Crozier USN," 22.

13. Chief of Naval Operations, *Command Investigation*, 487–90.

14. US Navy, "Witness Statement of CAPT Brett Crozier USN," 22.

15. US Department of Defense, "Transcript: Secretary of the Navy Braithwaite and Chief of Naval Operations Adm. Gilday Hold a Press Briefing on the Results of the USS Theodore Roosevelt Command Investigation, June 19, 2020," www.defense.gov/Newsroom/Transcripts/Transcript /Article/2227258/secretary-of-the-navy-braithwaite-and-chief -of-naval-operations-adm-gilday-hold/.

16. Paul Szoldra and Jeff Schogol, "New Emails Reveal the Chaotic Final Days of Brett Crozier's Command of the USS Theodore Roosevelt," *Task & Purpose*, September 18, 2020, https://taskandpurpose.com /news/navy-theodore-roosevelt-crozier-emails/.

17. US Navy, "FOIA Request," part 208, 92.

18. US Department of Defense, "Transcript: Secretary of the Navy Braithwaite and Chief of Naval Operations Adm. Gilday Hold a Press Briefing."

19. Chief of Naval Operations, *Command Investigation*, 1182.

20. Brett Odom, "The Navy's Monday-Morning Quarterback Investigation," *Proceedings*, June 2020, www.usni.org/magazines/proceedings /2020/june/navys-monday-morning-quarterback-investigation.

21. Chief of Naval Operations, *Command Investigation*, 1182.

22. US Navy, "Witness Statement of CAPT Brett Crozier USN," 21–22.

23. US Navy, "Witness Statement of CAPT Brett Crozier USN," 21–22.

24. US Navy, "Witness Statement of CAPT Brett Crozier USN," 18.

CONCLUSION

1. Adam Grant, *Think Again: The Power of Knowing What You Don't Know* (New York: Viking, 2021).

SELECTED BIBLIOGRAPHY

CHAPTER ONE: THE POWER OF "NO"

Alexander, John T. *Catherine the Great*. New York: Oxford University Press, 1988.

Alsop, Susan Mary. *Yankees at the Court: The First Americans in Paris*. New York: Doubleday, 1982.

Buell, Augustus. *Paul Jones, Founder of the American Navy: A History*. New York: Charles Scribner's Sons, 1903.

Chapelle, Howard I. *The History of the American Sailing Navy: The Ships and Their Development*. New York: Bonanza, 1949.

Cooper, James Fenimore. *History of the Navy of the United States of America*. Annapolis, MD: Naval Institute Press, [1856] 2001.

Golder, F. A. *John Paul Jones in Russia*. Garden City, NY: Doubleday, Page, 1927.

Morison, Samuel Eliot. *John Paul Jones: A Sailor's Biography*. New York: Time-Life, 1964.

Paullin, Charles. *Diplomatic Negotiations of American Naval Officers, 1778–1883*. Lancaster, PA: Johns Hopkins Press, 1912.

Pratt, Fletcher. *The Navy: A History*. New York: Garden City, 1941.

Russell, Phillips. *John Paul Jones: Man of Action*. New York: Brentano's, 1927.

Seitz, Don. *The Life and Letters of John Paul Jones*. New York: A. L. Burt, 1900.

Sweetman, Jack. *Great American Naval Battles*. Annapolis, MD: Naval Institute Press, 1998.

Thomas, Evan. *John Paul Jones: Sailor, Hero, Father of the American Navy*. New York: Simon & Schuster, 2003.

Tuchman, Barbara. *The First Salute*. New York: Knopf, 1988.

CHAPTER TWO: A YOUNG MAN'S GAME

Allison, Robert J. *Stephen Decatur: American Naval Hero, 1779–1820.* Amherst: University of Massachusetts Press, 2005.

De Kay, James Tertius. *A Rage for Glory: The Life of Commodore Stephen Decatur, USN.* New York: Free Press, 2004.

Guttridge, Leonard F. *Our Country, Right or Wrong: The Life of Stephen Decatur, the U.S. Navy's Most Illustrious Commander.* New York: Forge, 2007.

Leiner, Frederick. "'. . . The Greater the Honor': Decatur and Naval Leadership," *Naval History* 15, no. 5 (October 2001), 30–34.

Kilmeade, Brian, and Don Yaeger. *Thomas Jefferson and the Tripoli Pirates: The Forgotten War That Changed American History.* New York: Sentinel, 2015.

Toll, Ian W. *Six Frigates: The Epic History of the Founding of the U.S. Navy.* New York: W. W. Norton, 2008.

United States. Office of Naval Records and Library. *Naval Documents Related to the Quasi-War between the United States and France, Naval Operations.* 7 vols. Washington, DC: US Government Printing Office, 1935–38.

CHAPTER THREE: RISKY BUSINESS

Burrell, Brian. *Damn the Torpedoes: Fighting Words, Rallying Cries, and the Hidden History of Warfare.* New York: McGraw-Hill, 1999.

Duffy, James P. *Lincoln's Admiral: The Civil War Campaigns of David Farragut.* New York: Wiley, 1997.

Farragut, Loyall. *The Life of David Glasgow Farragut, First Admiral of the United States Navy: Embodying His Journal and Letters.* New York: Appleton, 1879.

Lewis, Charles Lee. *David Glasgow Farragut: Admiral in the Making.* Annapolis, MD: Naval Institute Press, [1941] 2014.

———. *David Glasgow Farragut: Our First Admiral.* Annapolis, MD: Naval Institute Press, [1943] 2014.

McPherson, James M. *War on the Waters: The Union and Confederate Navies, 1861–1865.* Chapel Hill: University of North Carolina Press, 2012.

Symonds, Craig L. *Lincoln and His Admirals.* New York: Oxford University Press, 2008.

———. *The Civil War at Sea.* New York: Oxford University Press, 2012.

CHAPTER FOUR: COOL HAND GEORGE

Dewey, George. *Autobiography of George Dewey.* New York: Charles Scribner's Sons, 1913. Reprinted with introduction and notes by Eric Smith. Annapolis, MD: Naval Institute Press, 1987.

Ellis, Edward. *Dewey and Other Naval Commanders*. New York: Hurst & Company, 1899.

Fiske, Bradley. *Admiral Dewey: An Appreciation*. Annapolis, MD: Naval Institute Press, 1917.

Johnson, Rossiter. *The Hero of Manila: Dewey on the Mississippi and the Pacific*. New York: D. Appleton and Company, 1899.

Halstead, Murat. *Life and Achievements of Admiral Dewey from Montpelier to Manila*. Chicago: Our Possessions, 1898.

Lawrence, William. *A Concise Life of Admiral George Dewey, U.S.N.* Boston: J. F. Murphy, 1899.

Smith, Fredrika Shumway. *George Dewey, Admiral of the Navy*. Chicago: Rand McNally, 1963.

Spector, Ronald. H. *Admiral of the New Empire: The Life and Career of George Dewey*. Baton Rouge: Louisiana State University Press, 1974.

CHAPTER FIVE: THE PROTECTOR

Cutrer, Thomas W., and T. Michael Parrish. *Doris Miller, Pearl Harbor, and the Birth of the Civil Rights Movement*. College Station: Texas A&M University Press, 2018.

Goodwin, Doris Kearns. *No Ordinary Time: Franklin and Eleanor Roosevelt: The Home Front in World War II*. New York: Simon & Schuster, 2013.

James, Rawn, Jr. *The Double V: How Wars, Protest, and Harry Truman Desegregated America's Military*. New York: Bloomsbury, 2014.

Klinkner, Philip A., and Rogers M. Smith. *The Unsteady March: The Rise and Decline of Racial Equality in America*. Chicago: University of Chicago Press, 2002.

Miller, Richard E. *The Messman Chronicles: African-Americans in the U.S. Navy, 1932–1943*. Annapolis, MD: Naval Institute Press, 2004.

Miller, Vickie G. *Doris Miller: A Silent Medal of Honor Winner*. Burnet, TX: Eakin Press, 1997.

Morehouse, Maggi M. *Fighting in the Jim Crow Army: Black Men and Women Remember World War II*. Lanham, MD: Rowman & Littlefield, 2007.

O'Neal, Bill. *Doris Miller: Hero of Pearl Harbor*. Burnet, TX: Eakin Press, 2007.

Takaki, Ronald T. *Double Victory: A Multicultural History of America in World War II*. Boston: Little, Brown, 2001.

CHAPTER SIX: THE WORLD WONDERS

Borneman, Walter R. *The Admirals: Nimitz, Halsey, Leahy, and King—the Five-Star Admirals Who Won the War at Sea*. New York: Little, Brown, 2012.

Cutler, Thomas. *The Battle of Leyte Gulf: 23–26 October 1944.* Annapolis, MD: Naval Institute Press, 1994.

Drury, Bob, and Tom Clavin. *Halsey's Typhoon: The True Story of a Fighting Admiral, an Epic Storm, and an Untold Rescue.* New York: Grove, 2007.

Hornfischer, James. *The Last Stand of the Tin Can Sailors.* New York: Bantam, 2004.

Morison, Samuel Eliot. *Leyte, June 1944—January 1945,* vol. 12 of *History of United States Naval Operations in World War II.* Annapolis, MD: Naval Institute Press, [1958] 2011.

Potter, E. B. *Bull Halsey.* Annapolis, MD: Naval Institute Press, 1985.

Spector, Ronald H. *Eagle Against the Sun: The American War with Japan.* New York: Vintage, 1985.

Toll, Ian W. *Twilight of the Gods: War in the Western Pacific, 1944–1945.* New York: Norton, 2020.

CHAPTER SEVEN: NO WAY OUT

Armbrister, Trevor. *A Matter of Accountability: The True Story of the Pueblo Affair.* New York: Coward-McCann, 1970.

Brandt, Ed. *The Last Voyage of the USS Pueblo.* New York: W. W. Norton, 1969.

Bucher, Lloyd M., and Mark Rascovich. *Bucher: My Story.* Garden City, NY: Doubleday, 1970.

Cheevers, Jack. *Act of War: Lyndon Johnson, North Korea, and the Capture of the Spy Ship Pueblo.* New York: NAL Caliber, 2013.

———. "The Pueblo Scapegoat." *Naval History* 28, no. 5 (October 2014). www.usni.org/magazines/naval-history-magazine/2014/october/pueblo -scapegoat.

Crawford, Don. *Pueblo Intrigue.* Wheaton, IL: Tyndale House, 1969.

Gallery, Daniel V. *The Pueblo Incident.* Garden City, NY: Doubleday, 1970.

House of Representatives. *Report of Special Subcommittee on the U.S.S. Pueblo of the Committee on Armed Services, House of Representatives Ninety-First Congress,* First Session, 1969. Washington DC: US Government Printing Office, 1969.

Lerner, Mitchell B. *The Pueblo Incident: A Spy Ship and the Failure of American Foreign Policy.* Lawrence: University Press of Kansas, 2002.

Liston, Robert A. *The Pueblo Surrender: A Covert Action by the National Security Agency.* New York: M. Evans, 1988.

Murphy, Edward R., Jr., and Curt Gentry. *Second in Command*. New York: Holt, Rinehart and Winston, 1971.

Newton, Robert E. *The Capture of the USS Pueblo and Its Effect on SIGINT Operations*. Fort Meade, MD: Center for Cryptologic History, National Security Agency, 1992. https://nsarchive2.gwu.edu/NSAEBB/NSAEBB278/US_Cryptologic_History—The_Capture_of_the_USS_Pueblo.pdf.

Schumacher, F. Carl, and George C. Wilson. *Bridge of No Return: The Ordeal of the U.S.S. Pueblo*. New York: Harcourt, Brace, Jovanovich, 1971.

Spaulding, Raymond C. *Some Experiences Reported by the Crew of the USS Pueblo and American Prisoners of War from Vietnam*. San Diego: Naval Health Research Center, 1975. www.history.navy.mil/research/library/online-reading-room/title-list-alphabetically/s/some-experiences-reported-crew-uss-pueblo-american-prisoners-war-vietnam.html.

CHAPTER EIGHT: PIRATES OF THE GULF OF ADEN

BBC News. "U.S. Captain Rescued from Pirates." April 13, 2009. http://news.bbc.co.uk/2/hi/africa/7996087.stm.

Phillips, Richard. *A Captain's Duty: Somali Pirates, Navy SEALs, and Dangerous Days at Sea*. New York: Hyperion, 2010.

Siegel, Robert. "Multi-National Task Force Focuses on Preventing Piracy." NPR, April 13, 2009. www.npr.org/templates/story/story.php?storyId=103054534.

US Navy. "Admiral Michelle Howard, Retired." www.navy.mil/Leadership/Biographies/BioDisplay/Article/2235996/admiral-michelle-howard.

Wyland, Scott. "U.S. Navy's 1st Female 4-Star Admiral Set to Retire." *Stars and Stripes*, September 26, 2017. www.stripes.com/news/us-navy-s-1st-female-4-star-admiral-set-to-retire-1.489556.

CHAPTER NINE: THE RED FLARE

Associated Press. "Teddy Roosevelt Captain Says He Knowingly Risked Career with Virus Warning." *Navy Times*, September 19, 2020. www.navytimes.com/news/your-navy/2020/09/19/captain-says-he-knowingly-risked-career-with-virus-warning/.

Chief of Naval Operations. *Command Investigation Concerning Chain of Command Actions with Regard to COVID-19 Onboard USS Theodore Roosevelt (CVN-71)*. Washington, DC: US Navy, June 19, 2020. https://assets.documentcloud.org/documents/7212256/TR-Command-Investigation-with-Appendices.pdf.

Chute, Nate. "'Sailors Do Not Need to Die': A Timeline of Coronavirus Spread on USS Theodore Roosevelt." *USA Today*, April 1, 2020. www .usatoday.com/story/news/2020/04/02/coronavirus-guam-coronavirus -cases-uss-theodore-roosevelt-news-updates/5108314002/.

Cohn, Lindsay, Alice Friend, and Jim Golby. "This Is What Was So Unusual About the U.S. Navy Making Captain Brett Crozier Step Down." *The Washington Post*, April 5, 2020. www.washingtonpost.com/politics /2020/04/05/this-is-what-was-so-unusual-about-us-navy-making -captain-brett-crozier-step-down/.

Gafni, Matthias. "Exclusive: Capt. Brett Crozier Explains Why He Sent Email Warning of Roosevelt Coronavirus Outbreak." *San Francisco Chronicle*, September 18, 2020. www.sfchronicle.com/bayarea/article /Exclusive-Capt-Brett-Crozier-explains-why-he-15576933.php.

Gafni, Matthias, and Dominic Fracassa. "Navy Won't Reinstate Capt. Crozier to Helm Coronavirus-Stricken Roosevelt Aircraft Carrier." *San Francisco Chronicle*, July 21, 2020 (updated). www.sfchronicle.com/bayarea/article /Navy-won-t-reinstate-Capt-Brett-Crozier-to-15352808.php.

Gafni, Matthias, and Joe Garofoli. "A Captain's Choice." *San Francisco Chronicle*, April 5, 2020. www.sfchronicle.com/nation/article/Capt-Crozier -The-man-who-risked-his-career-to-15179363.php.

Gafni, Matthias, and Joe Garofoli. "Exclusive: Captain of Aircraft Carrier with Growing Coronavirus Outbreak Pleads for Help from Navy." *San Francisco Chronicle*, March 31, 2020. www.sfchronicle.com/bayarea /article/Exclusive-Captain-of-aircraft-carrier-with-15167883.php.

Graff, E. J. "These Were Our 10 Most Popular Posts of 2020." *The Washington Post*, December 31, 2020. www.washingtonpost.com/politics/2020/12 /31/these-were-our-10-most-popular-posts-2020/.

Harkins, Gina. "6 Big Takeaways from the Full Navy Investigation into a Carrier's COVID Outbreak." Military.com, September 19, 2020. www.mili tary.com/daily-news/2020/09/19/6-big-takeaways-full-navy-investigation -carriers-covid-outbreak.html.

Korb, Lawrence. "Officials Continue to Throw Capt. Brett Crozier Under the Bus for Outbreak on Navy Carrier." *Military Times*, June 28, 2020. www .militarytimes.com/opinion/commentary/2020/06/28/officials -continue-to-throw-capt-brett-crozier-under-the-bus-for-outbreak -on-navy-carrier/.

LaGrone, Sam. "Carrier Roosevelt CO Asks Navy to Quarantine Entire Crew Ashore as COVID-19 Outbreak Accelerates." US Naval Institute News, March 31, 2020. https://news.usni.org/2020/03/31/carrier-roosevelt-co -asks-navy-to-quarantine-entire-crew-ashore-as-covid-19-outbreak -accelerates.

———. "Carrier Roosevelt CO Relieved Over 'Extremely Poor Judgment' in Creating 'Firestorm' Over COVID-19 Outbreak." US Naval Institute News, April 2, 2020. https://news.usni.org/2020/04/02/carrier-roosevelt -co-relieved-over-extremely-poor-judgement-in-creating-firestorm-over -covid-19-outbreak.

———. "TR Investigation Fallout: Crozier Won't Be Reinstated, Strike Group CO Promotion Delayed." US Naval Institute News, June 19, 2020. https://news.usni.org/2020/06/19/tr-investigation-fallout-crozier-wont -be-reinstated-strike-group-co-promotion-delayed.

———. "Almost 600 Sailors on Carrier Roosevelt Have Tested Positive for COVID-19." US Naval Institute News, April 12, 2020. https://news.usni .org/2020/04/12/almost-600-sailors-on-carrier-roosevelt-have-tested -positive-for-covid-19.

LaGrone, Sam, and Ben Werner. "UPDATED: Modly Resigns Amidst Carrier Roosevelt Controversy; Army Undersecretary to Serve as Acting SEC-NAV." US Naval Institute News, April 7, 2020. https://news.usni.org /2020/04/07/modly-offers-resignation-amidst-carrier-roosevelt -controversy.

Odom, Brett, "The Navy's Monday-Morning Quarterback Investigation." Proceedings, June 2020. www.usni.org/magazines/proceedings/2020/june /navys-monday-morning-quarterback-investigation.

Peniston, Bradley. "The Battle of USS Theodore Roosevelt: A Timeline." Defense One, April 7, 2020. www.defenseone.com/threats/2020/04/timeline -battle-uss-theodore-roosevelt/164408/.

Schogol, Jeff. "Emails Reveal How Capt. Crozier's Pleas for Help from the Navy Fell on Deaf Ears until His Bombshell Letter Leaked." Task & Purpose, October 27, 2020. https://taskandpurpose.com/news/crozier -theodore-roosevelt-emails-navy.

Szoldra, Paul, and Jeff Schogol. "New Emails Reveal the Chaotic Final Days of Brett Crozier's Command of the USS Theodore Roosevelt." Task & Purpose, September 18, 2020. https://taskandpurpose.com/news/navy -theodore-roosevelt-crozier-emails/.

"Timeline: Theodore Roosevelt COVID-19 Outbreak Investigation." US Naval Institute News, June 23, 2020. https://news.usni.org/2020/06/23 /timeline-theodore-roosevelt-covid-19-outbreak-investigation.

US Department of Defense. "Transcript: Secretary of the Navy Braithwaite and Chief of Naval Operations Adm. Gilday Hold a Press Briefing on the Results of the USS Theodore Roosevelt Command Investigation, June 19, 2020." www.defense.gov/Newsroom/Transcripts/Transcript/Article/22 27258/secretary-of-the-navy-braithwaite-and-chief-of-naval-operations -adm-gilday-hold/.

SELECTED BIBLIOGRAPHY

US Navy. "FOIA Request DON-NAVY-2020-00648, Parts 201–209." Requested by Paul Szoldra on April 3, 2020. www.muckrock.com/foi/united-states-of-america-10/emails-from-capt-brett-crozier-91301/#comms.

US Navy. "Witness Statement of CAPT Brett Crozier USN." Given May 8, 2020. https://assets.documentcloud.org/documents/7212572/USS-Theodore-Roosevelt-Coronavirus-Crozier.pdf.

INDEX